This Private Edition of *Moving the Hat*, published by Calling Crow Press—the text is not professionally proofed, so all my typos, gaffes, and bad grammar are present in their radiant glory—printed for presentation purposes and not for resale, consists of fifteen copies only, of which the book in your hands is number

Moving the Hat

A Literary Memoir

Richard Snodgrass

Calling Crow Press

Pittsburgh

Also by Richard Snodgrass

Fiction

There's Something in the Back Yard

The Books of Furnass

All That Will Remain

Across the River

Holding On

Book of Days

The Pattern Maker

Furrow and Slice

The Building

Some Rise

All Fall Down

Redding Up

Torn

Books of Photographs and Text

An Uncommon Field: The Flight 93 Temporary Memorial

Kitchen Things: An Album of Vintage Utensils

Memoir

The House with Round Windows

Moving the Hat

Move the hat; moving the hat—expressions used by construction inspectors in San Francisco during the 1960s and '70s to express the activity of moving on, moving around, to get on with it; as in after a coffee break: "Time to go move the hat."

Copyright © 2025 by Richard Snodgrass

All rights reserved. In accordance with the U.S. Copyright Act of 1976, the scanning, uploading, and electronic sharing of any part of this book without the permission of the author constitute unlawful piracy and theft of the author's intellectual property.

Published by Calling Crow Press
Pittsburgh, Pennsylvania

Book design by Book Design Templates, LLC

Printed in the United States of America
ISBN 979-8-9914269-1-6
Library of Congress Catalog Control Number: 2025913515

For my family;

And, of course,

as with all things,

for Marty.

Your love is equal to what you'll do for it.

Moving the Hat

Moving the Hat

On the camera's groundglass, One-Eyed Teddy looks back at me, friendly, jovial, all open-arms and happy smiles. He sits in the light tent I've set up in the basement, twin spotlights outside the tent beaming down, creating the soft light that goes everywhere. I would prefer to use my Rollei 2 ¼ Single Lens Reflex, but I'm in my eighties now, even a 2 ¼ is too much to manipulate these days—much less a view camera—I make do with my trusty Nikon D90, the groundglass at the rear masked off with black tape to simulate the square format I will crop down to on the computer. The hours spent under safelights in the darkroom long past.

I'm sitting on a low stool, my head under a darkcloth—old habits run deep—studying the composition—"Hi Teddy, may I take your image?"—making minute adjustments to the camera angle, the height of the tripod, so I don't hear my wife Marty when she comes up behind me.

"I was wondering where Teddy got to," she says, a disembodied voice that makes me jump a foot. "He wasn't in his rocking chair in the living room. Sorry, didn't mean to scare you."

When I look up from under the cloth, the expression on her face is anything but sorry. She obviously thinks it's a good joke.

"You need to honk your horn next time," I say.

"That would probably scare you even more. So, what's all this? A new book?"

"Well, I've been gathering these old toys for a while, trying to figure out what to do with them. So, I thought I'd just go ahead as if I knew what I was doing."

"Not knowing what you were doing as you started out never stopped you before."

"Sometimes I think the reason I write the books or take photographs is to find out what the hell interests me so much that I would go to all the time and trouble to do it."

"As good a reason as any other," Marty says, always the pragmatist.

I stick my head back under the darkcloth, confront One-Eyed Teddy again. Maybe he's too happy, too jovial. Why would you be so jolly having lost an eye? But you never know until you see the actual exposure. I take the image, bracketing to give me options in the processing.

Richard Snodgrass

Moving the Hat

After I take the image, I change Teddy's position, move the camera closer. Now it's a different Teddy. Not so happy with his affliction. More considered. I take the new image, then follow Marty upstairs to the kitchen. As she starts prepping vegetables in the sink for dinner, I say,

"I've got an idea how to use these photographs of vintage toys. Jack thinks I should include them in a book called *Snippets of a Snodgrass*. A follow-up to my earlier memoir, *The House with Round Windows*. That book talked about my early relationship to my older brother and the family. This one would take it up through the present."

Marty brushes a stray hair off her forehead with the back of her wrist. "I like the idea, but you need a better title than *Snippets*. I love Jack but. . . ."

"It would be in short prose sections, each one with an attending image. Like I used in my other prose-and-image books. Jack said it would be like us drinking Guinness at the Harp & Fiddle, me telling stories."

"And the images of the toys? You once called them *Childish Things*."

"Metaphors for the prose passages. Along with some of my other images, snapshots, documents."

"That could work," Marty says, putting spinach and arugula in the vegie drier and setting it to spinning. "But what's your story line? And don't tell me it's about your relationship with De. I'm sick and tired of you trying to write about your famous brother."

"Me too."

"Besides, he ended up wanting to kill you." She divides the green into our salad bowls, starts adding tomato slices, olives, sardines.

"De was always over-dramatic. No, I think a better story is how I've tried to establish myself as a person without him, or maybe despite him, and become an artist in my own right."

"That would cover the *Snippets* of Jack's idea. But what about the Snodgrass part? How does that play into it?"

"One of the challenges of accepting myself was learning how to live with a ridiculous name like Snodgrass."

"Tell me about it," Marty says. She stacks the bowls of salad along with a bread plate up her arm, waitress-style, while carrying the bottle of salad dressing, napkins, and silverware in the other, nodding for us to go into the dining room. "You could say it's all a matter of balance."

Richard Snodgrass

Moving the Hat

A wifely joke, that. Mentioning a matter of balance. Because at the age of eighty--four, I have no balance. None. Zilch. Well, very little. Put me in an empty space, with nothing for me to brace myself, and I can stand there maybe three seconds before I topple over. It's not that the room starts to spin as with vertigo. It's simply that you fall over. You have no way to determine which way is up. Timber, as Marty will say as I go careening through the house.

Twenty years earlier, flying into San Francisco, my right ear never unpopped. After several weeks of much heavy swallowing, tilting my head and thumping it with the heel of my hand like you do after swimming, I went to the doctor. He ran a series of tests and informed me that I had suffered a condition called Sudden Hearing Loss I said, No Kidding. He told me that in addition to increased problems with my hearing as I got older, I would also have problems with my balance because of the changes to my inner ear. I figured, Oh sure, and pretty much forgot about it until ten years later when I found I was having trouble keeping upright and got myself a cool walking stick.

The problem of maintaining my balance got me thinking that everything in the known universe depends on the balance between opposites. The universe as we know it is filled with two types of energy, positive and negative. Positive energy is heat and the force of creation, while negative energy is cold and the force of destruction. Neither one is good nor bad, they are just there. However, the laws of physics, data from experiments, and common sense tells us that the overall electrical charge of the universe is zero. One force balances against the other. There is exactly as much positive electric charge in the universe as there is negative electric charge. Scientists call this the zero-energy universe because one works against the other. In other words, they maintain their balance. In order to exist.

And it's not just the physical world that depends on balance. Light and dark; right and wrong; young and old; soft and hard; up and down. The list goes on. Each provides the opposition to define the other.

"I'll take your word for it," Marty says, handing me a dishtowel. "So what's the balance involved living with a name like Snodgrass?"

Richard Snodgrass

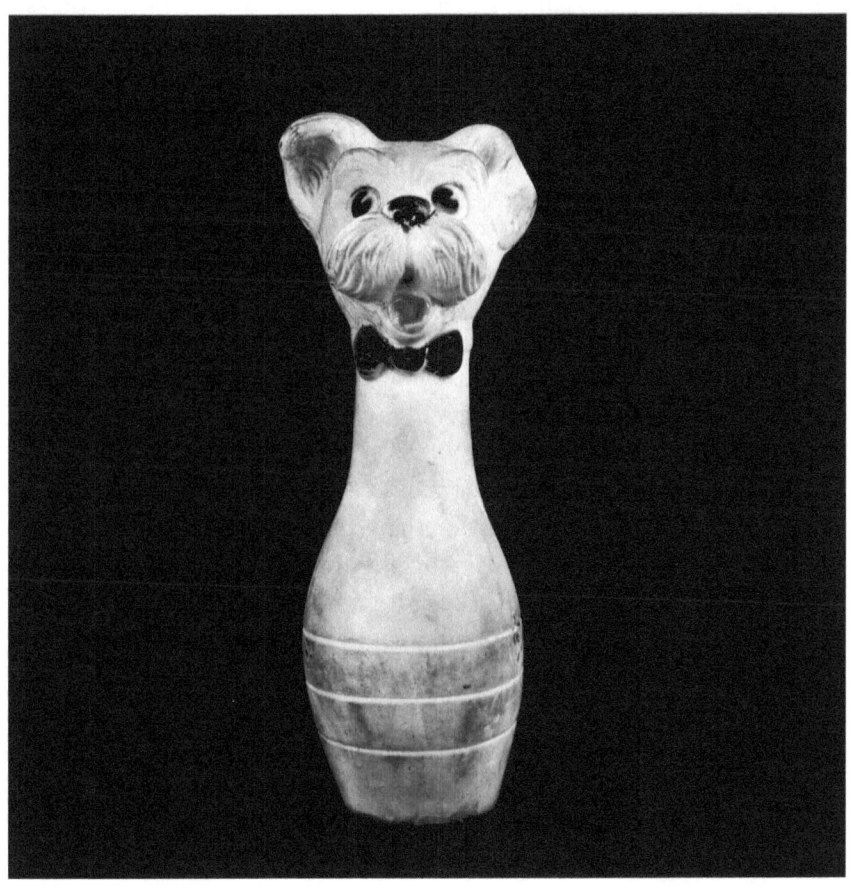

Moving the Hat

To a Snodgrass, the name connotes sophistication, learning, even a touch of the aristocratic. Eventually, however, the realization sets in that most of the world thinks the name is downright silly. Balancing those two viewpoints can be quite a high-wire act.

The story goes, at least as far my family is concerned, that the name originated in Ayrshire when a man named Snod was given a fiefdom for services in the Crusades, a piece of land that came to be known as Snod's grass. Get it? The word *Snod* in Middle English is an adjective meaning smooth; it seems it is also a verb that means to castrate. Something I used it on jobsites when I was a construction inspector and an ironworker would amble up my first day on a project: "Snodgrass, what kind of a name is that?" "Lowland Scot," I'd say, then tell him the derivation, making a snipping gesture with two fingers as I told him the castration part. Funny, I never had comments about my name after that.

There have been few famous Snodgrasses besides my Pulitzer Prize-winning brother, W. D. Mostly the name has been used for comic purposes, usually ascribed to overblown, pompous fictional characters. Dickens probably started it with August Snodgrass in Pickwick Papers, a young, overbearing, innocuous fellow who declares himself a poet though he never writes anything. Mark Twain picked up the name for a brief series of travel articles entitled The Thomas Jefferson Snodgrass Letters, one of his first attempts to write in a vernacular voice. Pongo Snodgrass appeared in the British comic magazine, *Whizzer and Chips*; Mr. Snodgrass was a frequent blustery character in the American comic strip Grin N Bear It. We fared better—though not by much— in Ogden Nash's poem, "Are You a Snodgrass, Too?" Nash divided people into two categories: kindly amiable Snodgrasses and the devious Swozzlers who spend their lives duping them, the premise being, I suppose, that's it's alright to be a victim as long as it's cute, though I don't buy it. I grew up hearing Stretch Snodgrass on the radio show, "Our Miss Brooks." But by far, my favorite use of the name appears in a science fiction story, "Snodgrass and Other Illusions," by Ian MacLeod, where John Lennon—yes, that John Lennon—gets tired of playing with the Beatles and lives a fantasy life as a civil servant named, you guessed it, Snodgrass.

Richard Snodgrass

"So, what are thinking of calling this book? You've got the balance theme working for you but a title like *A Matter of Balance* sounds dry as stale toast—"

"Stale toast?"

"It was the first thing I could think of. I had some toast earlier and it was. . .really dry. Don't change the subject. And you know what I think of any title with the name Snodgrass in it. Yuk! Who would want to read something like that?"

"I was thinking, Look, Look, Says Dick."

"No."

"Now hold on. Let me tell you how I got there. I started out with *Tales of a Storyteller*, then I thought *Fiction and Fact from Dick's Almanac*, or maybe *Let me Tell You a Story*—"

"No, no, and no."

"What about, *Coming in from Behind*, a sort of double entendre...."

I get the look.

"I was only kidding. With any of them."

"I would hope so."

"Okay, seriously: I'm calling it *Moving The Hat*. Because that's what I was doing all those years, chasing the dream. The hat seems to represent to me the adult persona I established for myself from my experiences working as a construction inspector, and then I set out moving the hat around, back and forth across the country all those years, trying to establish myself as an artist—for that matter, trying to discover what that art was, writing or photography."

"Sounds worth a try. Let's see what you can do with it."

"Or, maybe *Run, Spot. Run*. Or *Fun with Dick and Jane. Fun with Dick and Marty*?

Run, Dick, Run!

Richard Snodgrass

"And you're going to keep your brother out of it? Because you've tried to tell your story with him before, and it never worked."

Tried four times—with titles such as *Brother Mine*, *Oh Brother*, *Song of a Poet*—but who's counting? Marty, apparently. I wanted the book to pick up the story begun in my earlier memoir, *The House with Round Windows*, taking my relationship with my brother from when I was in college and he was a major influence, through my later years when I started to question a number of the precepts on which he based his life and work. Our estrangement reached a climax when he blamed me for the breakup of his third marriage. Well, there are many sides to any story. For years I thought the story of the decline of our relationship would make a good literary story, helping to explain my brother's later ideas and poetry. But eventually it dawned on me that I really didn't know that much about my brother's later ideas and poetry, and there might be other intentions behind my wanting to tell that story.

"The man did you no favors, Dick. I'm not sure he ever did."

"He was central to my early education and thinking. And any story about me would have to take that into account. But I know now he's not the focus. That would be me."

"About time," Marty mutters, then smiles, another kind of joke, as she puts the salad bowls in the cupboard.

The House with Rounf Windows tells the story of the death of our sister Barbara, and De's conclusion that she willed her death because she had nothing to live for as a result of my parent's emotional games. That formed the basis of his early poetry and esthetics, and he laid them on me when I was a late teenager, successfully alienating me from my parents. For years I was an acolyte to the scripture of W. D. Snodgrass. Our relationship changed, however, when I began to learn the other side of my family's story, and De wouldn't tolerate any ideas that questioned his own.

Marty hangs up the dish towel, makes sure the stove is off, and leads the way to the living room. "What was it your mother said? Everything the family did was human."

"I wonder if she meant it as an acceptance or a lament."

"Probably both. She knew all about balance."

Richard Snodgrass

Moving the Hat

To be a guy with a name like Snodgrass, growing up in a Western Pennsylvania steel town, meant that you either had to be very tough or have a great sense of humor. My father, it seems, was of the former persuasion. Even though he was Doc Snodgrass' kid; as a teenager he worked on the ice wagon, where he and the driver fought other crews daily for the best blocks of ice; and he could hoist a block weighing hundreds of pounds into an ice chest. When I asked him about it, he pooh-poohed it, saying it was all in the balance. As for me growing up, at one time or another known as Snots, Snot-in-the-Grass, and, the most inventive, Booger-Weed, I laughed a lot.

Beaver Falls wasn't even that tough of a mill town. It was the last of a chain of steel towns running north from Pittsburgh along the Ohio and Beaver rivers; its mills primarily were involved with shaping rather than making steel, unlike towns closer to Pittsburgh like Aliquippa and Ambridge. Plus Beaver Falls had the genteel influence of Geneva College, one of the few Covenanter colleges in the country. My family was further removed from the grittier sections of town by living up on College Hill, a block from Geneva—the big orange brick house with curved (not round) windows and cement lions in front.

My father, Bruce DeWitt, born and raised in Beaver Falls, made something of himself as a certified public accountant, traveling daily by train to his office in Pittsburgh, Snodgrass & Company at one time being the largest independent accounting firms in the country. This in the days after World War II when the smoke was so heavy it turned daylight to nighttime and my father took an extra white shirt in his briefcase to change into after going out to lunch. My mother, Helen Murchie, a preacher's daughter originally from Red Oak, Iowa, in addition to raising four children, was variously the President of the School Board; President of the College Hill Women's Club, an airplane spotter standing on top of the Broadhead Hotel scanning the sky for the Luftwaffe; and prime genealogist and eventually Regent of the local chapter of the Daughters of the American Revolution. I guess it fair to say, in addition to the funny name, we weren't your representative family in Beaver Falls, Pennsylvania.

Richard Snodgrass

Moving the Hat

WORDS MY FATHER LIVED BY

There were three men in a boat and the oars leaked.
A relatively common saying, in one variation or another, in the early 20th Century, said by my father as a comment on a perplexing situation or his general consternation at things.

Pigs off the diamond.
A baseball expression, from the time my father was a minor league catcher and unpenned pigs would wander out on the playing field; used whenever any animal was where it shouldn't be, such as a cat on his worktable or a dog on his shoe.

Every day in every way I keep getting better and better.
A quote from Émile Coué, a French psychologist, hypnotist, and writer who introduced a popular method of self-improvement based on optimistic autosuggestion.

You better get Wildroot Cream Oil, Charlie.
From a radio commercial he recited each morning as he slicked his hair down with the tonic. I can still smell the clean white lanolin.

We get along like two strange bulldogs in an alley.
An expression used by my father to describe his relationship with his youngest son. I don't know why.

I must be up and doing with a will for any fate.
A paraphrase of Longfellow's "Psalm of Life"; words that apparently helped to keep him going.

Whatever it is, the answer is no; whatever you want, you can't have it.
Always said with his businessman's smile, but I think he meant it.

Richard Snodgrass

Moving the Hat

I imagine my mother—a couple of years out of college, teaching Latin and the Classics (as well as coaching the basketball team; she had never played basketball in her life, much less coached it; still they won the state championship that year) in a Nebraska high school—must have thought she got an upgrade when the letter came from her secretly married husband that his family, that of a prominent doctor in a Western Pennsylvania town called Beaver Falls, was bringing her back east to live with them. I can imagine her excitement packing her bags, saying goodbye to her own family, her anticipation getting on the train. Then the start of her misgivings as she left the sun and cornfields of the American Midwest and approached the steel country around Pittsburgh, Pennsylvania, entered the world of smoke and soot and flaming mills described as "Hell with the lid off." I can imagine the sickness in her heart as she met and got to know the Snodgrass family, which from what I can gather was very much a Hell with the lid on.

My father's family, the family of Doctor Snodgrass, was prominent all right, but its viewpoint was definitely looking backward, not forward to the modern world developing after World War I. Doc Snodgrass' wife was a Victorian lady in the age of the flapper; though dressed winter and summer in black dresses that buttoned up from her toes to her neck, Catherine Fullmer Snodgrass definitely wore the pants in the family. No one moved in that household without Mother's approval, and Mother's approval was hard to come by. For instance, she wouldn't allow the good doctor to modernize his office with white walls and fixtures as was becoming the standard, his office had to remain looking like somebody's sunporch. What's more, she sat in the waiting room during office hours, making her own diagnoses of the patients. You can imagine how she treated her wayward son's secretly married wife, a farm girl at that, without the basic knowledge of the social graces befitting a proper wife—say, how to set a table, was the knife facing left or right? Disgraceful. Most dinnertimes were given to Mother Snodgrass berating shy Helen about my mother's latest transgressions and shortcomings. And my father, the tough guy, never spoke up to defend her. It seemed he was constitutionally unable to go against Mother.

Richard Snodgrass

Moving the Hat

When my father finally, after 57 attempts, got a position as an accountant with a firm east of Pittsburgh, he and my mother moved to Wilkinsburg, thirty-five miles away from Beaver Falls where they started their family. But my father insisted on returning to Beaver Falls every weekend, traveling the four-hour-plus journey by bus and trolley, my mother cradling her newborn baby. A few years later when he landed a position in Pittsburgh, he wasted no time in moving his family back to Beaver Falls, living a few doors away from his mother. Sigh. Eventually, when he started his own firm and it did well, my mother found the big house on College Hill and bought it while Father was away on business. There she made her stand, and with DeWitt's parents finally died off, could build a family the way she thought it should be, had always dreamed of. A house full of culture and the arts. A house where classical music played on the radio and phonograph. Where bookshelves lined the walls. Where cement lions and planters could flank the front steps.

My father was an intelligent man, the kind of intelligence that could play half a dozen people at chess at one time, blindfolded, that could add and subtract tall columns of precise figures and get precise answers, but he doesn't seem to have been particularly smart; he was intelligent enough to read and understand Spinoza, but was unable to grasp how the ideas could shape and change his life. My mother, on the other hand, was as intelligent as my father, probably more so, though in an age when women weren't supposed to be; and she was also smart, a kind of street smart, adding feeling and emotion to the mix. She was smart enough to know, for instance, when her husband forced her to live under his mother's thumb, that she was getting screwed in more ways than one. When she finally got her big house and could establish her world as she saw fit, it included the ability to raise at least one of her children, her fourth, without her in-laws looking over her shoulder criticizing everything she did. She was finally able to affirm her chosen purpose as a woman and mother. Child-rearing as an act of assertion. That would be Me.

Richard Snodgrass

Moving the Hat

In my neighborhood on College Hill, for all the family's prominence, my friends and playmates were the sons and daughters of steel workers, a bartender, bakery drivers, a bus driver, a postman, a teacher, milkman, and assorted professionals. I was the rich kid who owned the football and basketball, whose father organized pick-up softball games in our backyard so Dickie could have a chance to play. Most of the kids accepted me as I was—with an additional nicknames of Tex because I loved wearing cowboy boots even at that age—though there was something about me that Chicken Emrick couldn't stomach and he chased me flailing the belt for his paper route every chance he got.

Our house itself, with all the hallmarks of a brick mansion, sitting on its corner terrace, stuck out from the surrounding small frame and insulbrick-covered houses. But the inside was even more of a departure. Where the homes of my friends often had linoleum floors, easy chairs and sofas leaking springs and stuffing, bent-tube tables and chairs, our house had oriental carpets and tapestries, chandeliers and tasseled drapes, wainscoting and beamed ceilings, a large stained-glass window at the top of the oak staircase. Though for all our grandeur, for several years in the early fifties I had to go to the Munteans on Sundays to see *Super Circus* and *The Magical World of Disney* because my parents thought this new thing called television would never last. When we did get a television, it was the largest in the neighborhood, of course, and encased in a mahogany cabinet with doors embossed with an oriental scene (as it was known in those days) featuring a pagoda, a coolie, and a dragon.

My parents, mostly my mother, made sure that her four children—in order: William DeWitt, Barbara Helen, Shirley Ann, and the baby, Richard Bruce, known as Dick or Dickie—had as many cultural benefits as we could stand. That was particularly true by the time I came along, when my father was quite successful with his certified public accounting firm. Trips to Pittsburgh to the Carnegie Museum to see The International and the permanent collection, the Civic Light Opera, concerts by Andreas Segovia and the Pittsburgh Symphony. The arts were early on a part of my life. A way of life.

Richard Snodgrass

Moving the Hat

It seems the way that the lessons of the world are imparted to a child is as important as the lessons themselves. It certainly has a bearing on the degree the lessons stick. My father never sat me down for a talk, he instilled most of what he taught me—mainly how to navigate the channels of commerce, restaurants, check-ins, business dealings—through osmosis, watching him in action. I was surprised in my mid-thirties how thoroughly those lessons were ingrained in me when I was thrown into managing a seven-office company, and I knew intuitively how to handle every circumstance—I realized at one point that I was handling situations with employees, suppliers, clients exactly the way my father would. On the other hand, my mother's lessons were more of a personal nature, how to treat others—the basics of kindness and politeness—how to treat myself, depend on myself, play the hand you're given, get on with whatever it is your doing, be independent. My father's cautionary words to my mother: "Helen, if you're going to teach them to think for themselves, you can't blame them when they do."

My older sisters, Barbara and Shirley, as older sisters will, provided much of my day-to-day learnings—teaching me everyday skills such as tying my shoelaces, how to build Tinkertoys and Lincoln Logs, as well as reading to me the *Wizard of Oz* books. They were also—unintentionally, of course—my introductions to sex. The actual talk about the birds and the bees came one evening from my neighbor, Joe Mulroy, sitting on his front steps when I was twelve or so; I commented that Tootsie Muntean sure must have hurt when that baseball hit her in the balls, and Joe informed me that Tootsie Muntean didn't have balls. Now, I must have known such a thing some time earlier, as a toddler I usually took my baths with one sister or another, but at the time it seemed a revelation. Actually, I spent most of my childhood trying to see my sisters naked, on their way to and from the bathroom, peeking through door cracks and keyholes. The one time on a vacation when I was fourteen that I lay in bed with Barbara—all innocent enough, I suppose, though now I wonder—I was so excited or maybe scared that I threw up and ran a fever and she had to nurse me the rest of the night.

Richard Snodgrass

Moving the Hat

It was De, as an older brother will, who provided me an example of how to live. Which was ironic because he left for the service when I was four, and except for a couple years on his return finishing up at Geneva, was never around. It is doubly ironic because it seems De hated me. Unequivocally. Couldn't stand me. Refused to touch me. Though as he once recounted in an interview, he tried his best to harm me. I was only a few months old, Mother had put me in a baby carriage, and she told De not to rock it, that I could fall out the front end. But rock it he did, violently back and forth, and out I went, right on my head. He admitted in telling the story that it was a wonder I wasn't seriously hurt, my fontanel probably wasn't fully closed. But then De had a history of trying to damage his siblings, once tempting his beloved sister Barbara to lean out a third story window, just to see what would happen.

Mother thought De's aversion to me started when she was pregnant and the older, tougher boys kidded him about the visual proof that his mother was...er, getting fucked; not being a tough boy himself, he took it out on the visual proof. Possible, but I think it equally true that he resented the new fair-haired boy taking up his mother's affection. De had always been the star of the family, in the spotlight, the center of attention. But, unaware of his feelings, I took him as a role model as someone who was an artist, living a life in art. When he came back from the service, the house was full of his attempts to find his art form: a set of timpani in the living room; a cello on the sunporch; stacks of choral music on the baby grand piano; cardboard stage maquettes on the dining room table. When he went off to the Iowa City Writers Workshop, where he first failed as a playwright but found his footing as a poet, there was much rejoicing in the Snodgrass household. I remember in grade school almost having a fight with Gary Javens on the playground when I repeated my mother's comment that my brother was going to be the next Shakespeare. Neither one of us really knowing who Shakespeare was.

Richard Snodgrass

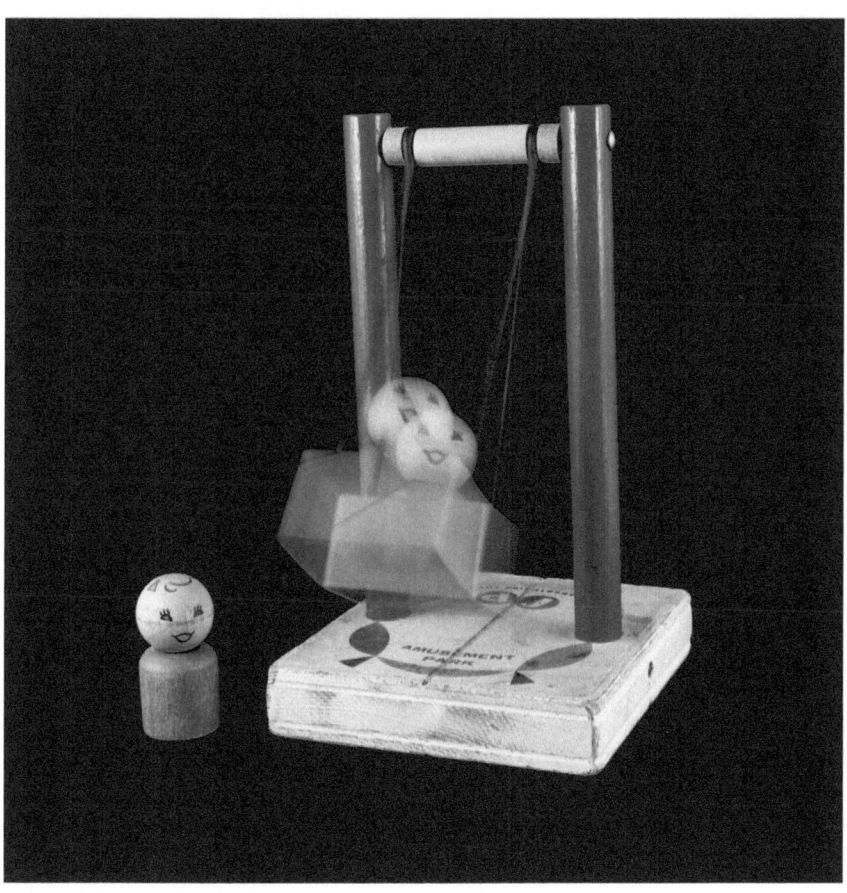

Moving the Hat

I will never know at this point whether I was a mistake or an intention; whether I was an accident, an unplanned by-product of my parents middle-age sex, or part of a plan (and a gamble) to even out the number of children, a second boy to match the two girls. Because in one way, I was the agent of balance in the family, a counterweight, the weight as it were that applies an opposite force to provide balance and stability in a mechanical system, if that's how you care to think of a family; on the other hand, I was a disrupter, an agent provocateur that prevents something, especially a system or process or event, all of which can be ascribed to that peculiar unit called a family, from continuing as usual or expected. It wasn't by accident, I figure, that my father crowned me as a toddler with the name The Baldy Sturber, as in the Bald Disturber, so named from my penchant I'm told for running around naked through the upstairs hall after my evening bath, avoiding all attempts to corral me. At times, it seems, a fitting image still.

All things considered, the Snodgrasses of Beaver Falls during the 1940s appear to have been a fairly typical American family, their civic oddities or anomalies evened-out, equally balanced:

$$well\text{-}to\text{-}do\ family = working\text{-}class\ mill\ town$$
$$old\ prominent\ name = new\ successful\ business$$
$$society\ page\ mentions = shot\text{-}and\text{-}a\text{-}beer\ neighbors$$

The event that permanently set the family cattywampus was when Barbara, the second child, the favorite daughter—in one view, the family's sacrificial lamb, the one subliminally chosen to be the glue of the family, which meant she would never have a life of her own, her personal happiness offered up on the altar of family love and devotion—woke up the morning of the Fourth of July in her twenty-seventh year, after a life of ill-health, plagued by asthma and allergies and a questionable heart, wheezing from the dust and soot she breathed. . .and died. Stopped breathing. Gone. Leaving those who were left to shift back and forth in compensation, try to achieve some stability, a balance that would never be found again, with lots of arm waving, tilting this way and that, trying to maintain some semblance of moving forward through Time while, Janus-like, always looking back.

Richard Snodgrass

Moving the Hat

When I was in high school, I was well on my way to follow in my brother's footsteps with playing the drums. I was the first-chair drummer in the marching band—though the truth is I faked it when it came to reading music—and was designated to play timpani in the orchestra, the height of prominence and achievement in the world of Beaver Falls percussionists. My future in music lay with "Colonel Bogey," "High School Cadets," "Stars and Stripes Forever."

Then one Sunday morning, when I decided to stay home from Sunday school and church, I turned on the television and found a program called *Look Up and Live*. Rather than some tv evangelist or heavy-handed sermon, the day's episode was called "The Theology of Jazz" and featured the Dave Brubeck Quartet. I had heard of jazz, of course, but that was Glenn Miller, Benny Goodman, Dixieland. I had never heard Modern Jazz. In the weeks that followed, the show presented Marion McPartland, more Dave Brubeck. After school I began to haunt the record shops in town, discovering Gerry Mulligan, Dizzy Gellespie, Bird. Shelley Mann, A new world opened up for me.

I began to take lessons at the local music store with a guy named Don Jasper. Don, in addition to teaching drums—he worked in the lab at the Tube Mill—played in a local quintet made up of other part-time musicians, guys who worked in clothing stores, the post office, laborers in the mills. Don was known throughout the region as the best drummer around, Art Blakeley and Miles would have him sit in when they came through Pittsburgh. After I learned the fundamentals, Don moved my lessons to his house so he could show me things on his drum set, let me play them for myself. We played records of Max Roach and Kenny Clark at half speed to figure out what they were doing. I practiced with two pencils in Latin class. I learned to keep time with my right hand on the ride cymbal and the off-beat with my left foot on the high-hat, add accents and breaks with my left hand on the snare, drop bombs with my right foot on the base drum. I lived the founding precept of modern jazz drumming: four-limb interdependence shall make you free.

Richard Snodgrass

Moving the Hat

When it was obvious I was serious about my drumming, my parents, no doubt at my mother's instigation, took me to Volkwein's in Pittsburgh where I picked out the most beautiful and expensive set of drums in the store—a Gretch outfit with the same size drums as Max Roach, along with Zildjian cymbals that were so crisp they made Don's teeth ache. It was a purchase I'm sure my father soon regretted, me thumping away long into the night in my attic room over their bedroom. For the next few years I continued my studies with Don while becoming the darling of high school proms and talent shows with drum solos—quite complex displays, actually, with different time signatures, a touch of comedy here and there, riffs taken from my idols. As a result I had new-found popularity, voted Most Liked in my Senior year, my own little posse. When my brother came for a visit, my mother insisted I show him my skills. De and I dutifully trooped to the attic where I showed him examples of modern drumming. Coming from the era of big bands, Gene Krupa, Buddy Rich, De didn't understand what was going on and was unimpressed. And said so. I was crushed.

With Don and his bandmates, I traveled on weekends to the jazz clubs in Pittsburgh to hear Blakely, Miles, early Coltrane. It was my introduction to the wider world, the life in clubs and the underworld, girls who lifted their skirts when the white guys went by. After I graduated from high school, Don told me that he had taught me everything he could, that it was time for me to load my drums in the car and go to New York or L.A. and pit myself against established pros. Well, I considered it for a time, but the reason I came up with for not doing so was that I didn't want to spend my life in dark smokey clubs. But I suspect there was another reason; I knew in my heart that, irrespective of what my brother said, I wasn't actually that good. The few times I played with other musicians I hopelessly rushed the beat; I didn't understand the basic role of a drummer: to keep accurate time. I never figured out the balance of being support and a driving force. I thought I was the show.

Moving the Hat

In truth there was a more decisive reason why I didn't set out to start my career as a jazz drummer: I didn't want to leave my girlfriend. With my new popularity in high school because of my drum solos, also came the attention of girls who would never look at me before. Including a pretty Italian girl named Joann. Ah Joann. Olive skin. Dark brown eyes. Thick curly brown hair. I could lose myself in her presence forever. Tried to.

It was during my time with Joann in my senior year that I had the life-changing visit with my brother in Rochester, NY, a visit and its aftermath I talk about in *The House with Round Windows* that I won't recount in detail here. Long story short: over several days my brother, aided by his second wife Jan, conducted what I assume they thought was a psychic intervention—begun from an innocent comment I made that I couldn't believe sometimes that my girlfriend loved me: Alarm! Alarm!—using the interrogation techniques De picked up in his psychoanalysis to lead me to the conclusions that my sister Barbara's death was from my parents' smother love, and that I was in danger of the same fate. Witness buying me the drum set. A car. Whatever I wanted. After those several days, I never looked at the world and people the same way. I learned to trust no one. To suspect the most innocent act of deadly consequences. That black could be white, white could be red. My brother's tutelage opened the world of art and literature and ideas for me; it gave me invaluable lessons in evaluating the happenings around me, taught me to stand up for myself, face problems head-on, be a problem-solver. It also made me terminally wary. Not always a bad thing, certainly.

Sadly, it also left me more dependent on my girlfriend than ever. With the love of my parents in question, I desperately needed her love. Always a recipe for disaster. I locked into her Italian family, so unlike my own, where people yelled at each other but got emotions over and done with, where feelings weren't hidden away but expressed. Imagine the surprise of that working-class barber and his wife, Joann's two older sisters and a baby brother, when they were beset by the youngest son of the well-to-do Snodgrass family. A cake-eater in their midst.

Richard Snodgrass

Moving the Hat

Joann's extended family lived down the valley in West Aliquippa, a small shoebox of a town, roughly eight blocks wide and a dozen blocks long, tucked in among the seven-mile-long Aliquippa works of J&L Steel, surrounded by the mill on two sides, the Ohio River, and the elevated railroad tracks, with only one way in or one way out, through a dark tunnel under the railroad tracks. "West," was made up primarily of Italians, with a smattering of Poles and Middle Europeans, the rhythms of the town determined by the cycles of the mills; at the change of shifts the men filed along the narrow streets, lunchpails under their arms, answering the calls of the sirens and whistles announcing the blows of the Besemer converters, the tapping of the blast furnace, the ring of steel on steel. At night you would walk out on the porch and the sky mounted high beyond the backyard or at the end of the block, roiling with clouds of smoke and steam flashing yellows and red and orange, no one paying any mind at an everyday occurrence.

Joann and her family traveled often to West for Sunday dinners, feast days, weddings and funerals, taking me along though I was never quite sure whether it was to show me off or show me up. Sitting around a dining room table, after tureens of wedding soup, plates of roast beef in tomato sauce, bowls of pasta and steamed vegetables, Joann's eight uncles would grill me to determine my intentions; at Christmas time they gave me my first double shot of whiskey, Crown Royal, and were as surprised as I was when I didn't fall out of my chair. One night I was led through a bar and down a back stairway to an unfinished basement, a few bare bulbs the only illumination along the rough whitewashed walls and exposed floor beams. Here the men of the Panthers Club chose sides and confronted each other in two long lines across the room. Tension was high as they sized each other up. Then one man from each side met in the center, circling slowly. At some signal or sign of advantage, each raised a clenched fist and threw it down, exposing a certain number of outstretched fingers as they shouted out their guess at the total.

"Quat-tro!"
"Cinque!"
"Se-i! Se-i! Se-i!"
I remember it was no game.

Richard Snodgrass

Moving the Hat

Joann's world was as foreign to me as could be. Just what I needed when I no longer trusted the world I was born into. And at the heart of the miracle and mystery of her new world was Holy Mother Church. I was raised United Presbyterian, the affiliation on both sides of my family going back generations; in fact, as noted earlier, my mother's father was a United Presbyterian minister in Iowa and Kansas; my parents met at a United Presbyterian school, Tarkio College; and being a United Presbyterian minister was traditionally only one of three career options open to Snodgrass males, the other two being either a doctor or a farmer. Needless to say, my newfound interest in Catholicism was not greeted warmly by the Snodgrasses of College Hill.

The most I knew about Catholics up to then was that they ate fish on Fridays, which was responsible for all the great fish fries in the taverns around town every week; they gave up things like candy and pies for Lent but beyond something to do with Easter I didn't understand the significance; they had a lot of children which meant they must believe in a lot of sex; and that we of the First United Presbyterian Church collectively disliked Catholics principally because every Sunday they took over the civic parking lot behind our church. My father actually couldn't say much about my new religious interest, because he never went to church himself. Every Sunday morning my mother drove my sisters and me downtown to Sunday school, then met us later for church. The thing was, my mother was always late meeting us again, the service had always started when we trailed in, Mother smiling and bustling about, adjusting her clothes. It took me until I was almost forty to realize Sunday mornings, after getting us kids out of the house, was when my parents had sex. God love 'em.

Joann's family never said I had to convert, but it was obvious that she wouldn't consider marriage if I didn't. But then no one had to make such a stipulation to me. Having lost the anchor of my family through De's talks, I was more than willing to accept into my life a beautiful sainted mother trailing form-revealing veils who greeted me with open arms and offered me succor. I was always particularly fond of that word: Succor.

"Wait a minute," Marty says. "Is this just some excuse to start talking about your brother again?"

"No, all I meant was that De's talks and letters unhinged my world to the point that I was desperate for some meaning and context. And Catholicism gave that to me. At least at the time."

"What did De think of Joann? Did he ever meet her?"

"He met her once. He didn't seem all that impressed."

Marty gives a self-satisfied smirk. As if she's just won something.

"Here's something he wrote to me in the summer of 1958:"

Now then, let me raise one real actual doubt about Joann as a personality for you — you must forgive me, but you know whose welfare I'm looking after. Does she have the real toughness which will almost certainly need? She is quite charming girl, from what I've seen. She is very, very handsome. But this, I confess, is a thing I distrust. What are her techniques? Are they ones that you can live with? Would I be wrong in guessing that the reason you've lost your happiness about into Pitt, and your excitement about possible careers you could enter, is that Joann is looking unhappy? . . . I had a pretty wife, once — one who looked unhappy most of the time. I became completely unable to accomplish anything. I ended up spending all my time winding around her ankles like a gelded cat, so she might smile and approve me. After seven years it still hadn't happened, we were more dependent upon each other than ever, more anxiously burrowing down into each other, each trying to make the other into the things that were lacking. . . .

Marty looks at me. "My case rests."

"Okay. I admit those are rather heavy ideas to lay on a vulnerable eighteen-year-old. But I was pretty much of a mess."

"So are most eighteen-year-olds. What he's talking about are things you only learn by living, not from pronouncements from on high."

"It didn't help, as I came to learn, that he ascribed to my vulnerabilities all his own deep dark monsters."

"Thank you."

Richard Snodgrass

Moving the Hat

I wanted to write since I first learned to write. In first and second grades I wrote supposed newspaper stories that my sainted sisters would type up for me and assemble into *The Snodgrass Tribune*, circulation 1. Like most little boys, I was interested in soldiers, though in my case it was the Praetorian Guard; somewhere I learned that a Roman legion once occupied an island, and I thought to write a novel about what their occupation of the place would be like, their interaction with the inhabitants. This was in the second grade, and I seemed to have already grasped writing as a way to understand how people lived. Early on, I had a love of counterpoint, how the different voices played off each other, and once I wrote an essay describing the ascending and descending swirls of a Bach fugue. But in high school, the impulse to write was overtaken by the impulse to photograph.

Now, admittedly, I backed into photography. In the mid-1950s, the photography annuals from magazines such as *Popular Photography* and *U.S. Camera* were one of the few places an overweight, pimply-faced teenager could find pictures of naked girls, and I built up quite a collection. But to my credit, I eventually turned the page. There I first encountered the work of Edward Weston and Cartier-Bresson, Ansel Adams and Walker Evans. When W. Eugene Smith published his landmark photo essay on Pittsburgh, I learned there was imagery to be found in places I knew. With the money I got for my sixteenth birthday, I purchased a Yashica Twin-Lens Reflex, being told that it was just as good as a Rollei. It wasn't, but the world opened up for me whenever I looked down into that luminous groundglass. Magic.

I drove everyone I knew half-crazy with my taking photographs, pictures of my friends and pets, pictures of soapy still-lifes, of Joann staring beatifically into a candle flame till her eyes watered, of her grandmother standing guard in a doorway watching where I put my hands. For a time I worked in local portrait and commercial studios where I learned the basics of film developing and printing, though I knew already I would never be satisfied taking yearbook photos, stacking wedding parties up flowered staircases for wedding albums, adjusting a drape around the shoulders of a nubile young woman, my fingers brushing flesh.

Richard Snodgrass

Moving the Hat

During the year I was at loose ends after graduating from high school I tried Geneva, but growing up a block from the campus I couldn't take it seriously. My time in the workforce, however, convinced me that I needed to go to college somewhere. In addition to apprenticing local photographers, I worked other jobs, including a service station attendant and clothing salesman, failing miserably at both. I came up with the idea to study photography at the Rochester Institute of Technology. RIT was the best school for photography in the country, though it was slanted heavily to the technical aspects of the medium. My problem with most schools, even the University of Pittsburgh, was that I didn't want to be away from Joann. At the time De was teaching at the University of Rochester, and I thought being close to him would override missing her. As it turned out I didn't have the science credits to get into RIT, and that ended that.

The job I liked best was the janitor at a catholic church and grade school in the neighboring town of New Brighton. As soon as classes were out in the afternoon, I roamed the big deserted building putting desks back in line, sweeping the old warped wood floors, cleaning the bathrooms—I had no idea little kids could be so dirty. I spent the final hours of my shift as well as all day Saturday in the church, waxing floors, polishing statues, just me and the Good Lord in his tabernacle, His humble servant. During the year I took Instruction, as it was called, from the monsignor at Joann's church, and was baptized one spring evening surrounded by Joann and her family. I attended daily Mass, me and a dozen little old ethnic ladies lining the back row, and made several pilgrimages to the Abby of Gethsemane in Kentucky, keeping the schedule with the Trappist monks as they chanted the Office seven hours a day. I still wanted to study photography but I thought I would get my college degree first, then pick up photography after. I found the solution of which school to go to in St. Vincent, a collage attached to a Benedictine Abby on the other side of Pittsburgh, close enough to see Joann on the weekends. I thought the choice would upset my father, but it turned out he was pleased, he told me a son of his going to St. Vincent would impress his Catholic clients.

Richard Snodgrass

Moving the Hat

It was so very like me: convert to Catholicism because of a girl, then get so engrossed in the religion that I thought seriously about becoming a monk. My motto, it seems: Everything in Excess.

From the time I started to consider St. Vincent, the idea danced around in my mind that, even though the worldly Benedictines were very different than the Trappists, the school would give me a taste of the monastic life, in case I decided to go that direction. Silly me. St. Vincent, sitting on a windy hilltop, most of the buildings of the monastery and college connected to the archabbey for tax purposes, gave me a taste of something but it wasn't religion. A majority of the students when I was there came from the mill towns of the Mon Valley, happy to be away from home, with little interest in studying. The guys on my floor had great fun rampaging about, sneaking in girls and beer, opening the windows at either end of the long hallway to create a wind tunnel in which to empty their wastepaper baskets, squatting on their roommates' desk to take a shit. Being considered a religious freak, getting up at five in the mornings to chant mass, I tended to be left alone. Most weekends I hitchhiked the sixty miles down the Turnpike to see Joann, but the times I stayed alone on campus, the chant of the schola carried down the long stone corridors.

When it was announced that my brother won the Pulitzer Prize for poetry, I received newfound notoriety at the school. But by far the most important event for me was the discovery of James Joyce's *Dubliners*. After reading a story in English class, that weekend during a snowstorm I hitchhiked into Pittsburgh to get a copy of the Viking paperback, a copy of which still sits on my desk. From that point on photography was put aside in favor of wanting to write about the life I knew in mill towns. When I informed the priest who taught the class of my intention, he told me not to get my hopes up, he hadn't seen in me any particular creativity. When I told De, he pooh-poohed it, aware himself of late development. Later I learned the good father had left the monastery to marry an ex-nun and was teaching high school somewhere in the Mon Valley.

Richard Snodgrass

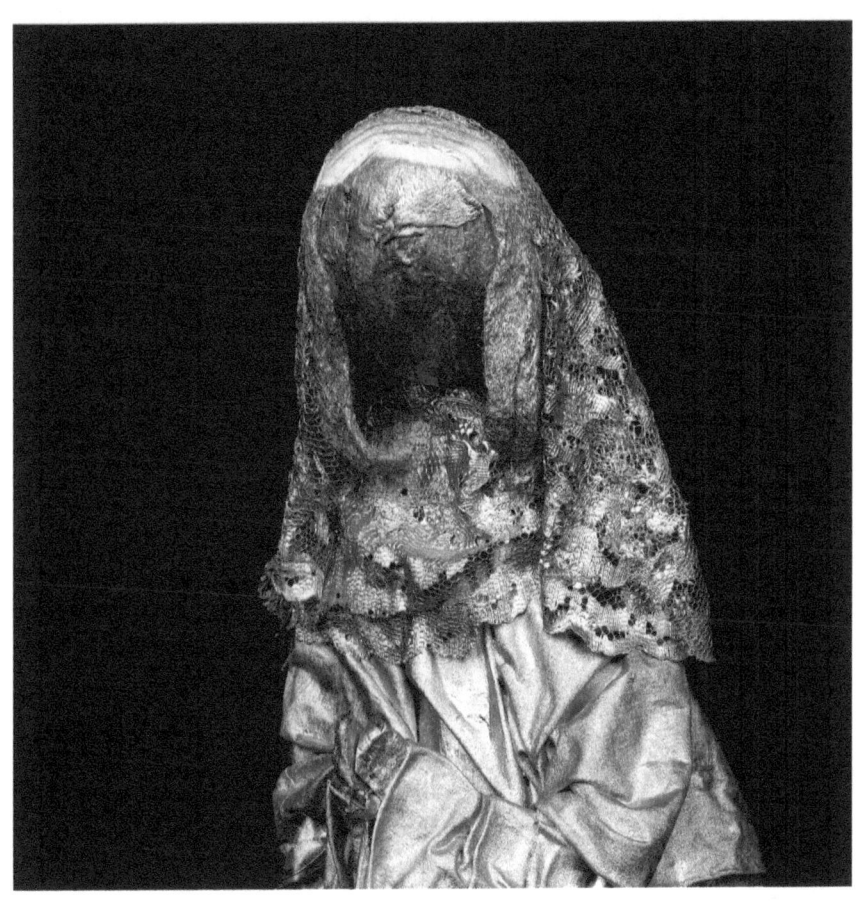

Moving the Hat

I wasn't very long at St. Vincent when I became all too aware that I wasn't going to make it as a monk. It was the start of the Sixties when girls' skirts were calf-length; but during my trips into Pittsburgh, even that six-inch glimpse of female ankle—to say nothing of my weekend necking with Joann—convinced me the monastic life wasn't for me. I decided that if I didn't have the makings of a priest, I would at least become a Catholic intellectual. Tada! And who better to instruct a budding Catholic scholar than the Jesuits. As it so happened, the University of Detroit was a Jesuit school, and De was teaching at a university a few miles away, Wayne State, where I could audit his classes on poetry. The best of all possible worlds.

Detroit was my coming of age—besides the fact that I turned twenty-one, the legal drinking age. After a feisty battle with the U of D administration, I was finally allowed to live off-campus. I found a second-floor apartment a half block from campus and with the help of Jan, my sister-in-law, learned how to set up a living arrangement for myself, learned how to navigate the mysteries of a supermarket and what utensils I needed, learned how to cook the basics. The apartment was on Dexter Avenue at Six Mile, and a bus line took into the black districts to jazz clubs where I heard Bill Evans and Miles and Cannonball, riding around in the middle of the night with never a problem, a different time. Two or three times a week I took another bus down Woodward to Wayne State where I sat at the back of De's classes. De was a charismatic and engaging teacher—totally in his element: in the spotlight, the center of attention—first reading a poem and then asking questions as to its meaning, leading his students like an analyst to draw things out they didn't know they knew. Frost. Eliot. Auden. Hardy. I learned more about the makings of literature in those classes that in all my other English classes combined. After class I would walk with him back to his office as an entourage of students buzzed around him, feeling privileged that I was the one he spoke to, though in time I became aware that he was always watching who was watching.

Richard Snodgrass

Moving the Hat

One summer evening—anxious to start my new life at U of D I took summer classes—I was crossing the main quad and came upon a rehearsal for the theater department's production of *Antony and Cleopatra*. Backstage a couple of guys were futzing around trying to tighten the head on a kettle drum. In an uncharacteristic gesture, I offered to help, showing them a few beat patterns. The director came running over to ask if I was a drummer and would I help the production. Thus, a star was born—or at least a bit player. I became the darling of the company with a host of new friends, female and male, and provided percussion for all the shows that summer. When fall came I was encouraged to take some acting classes, and I realized the others considered me a full-fledged member of the company. I was never an actor in a production, but when the directors learned I could develop complete suites for percussion—using the timpani, a snare drum and toms from the music department, a glockenspiel I found in a secondhand store, a dumbeck I bought in Greektown—I provided orchestration for all the productions that year, the principle one being Shakespeare's *Julius Ceasar*.

I dated a couple of the girls, though nothing serious; and one of the guys who was training as a ballet dancer invited me to join him as an extra when the traveling companies came to town. In that capacity I once carried the lead for the Royal Danis Ballet—balancing one corner of a wood platform as we hoisted her onstage for the finale—and for the Ballet Russe de Monte Carlo I was one of four assassins sent to avenge the Shah in *Scheherazade*. When one of us tripped over the backdrop and almost collapsed the scenery, a couple of enraged dancers chased us off the stage. Eventually the theater department, hard-up for candidates, tried to make me into a leading man—tall, slim, reasonably good looking, it was an easy mistake. However, a scene from Moliere showed I had no talent as a dramatic lead—until the department head came by and had me switch roles with the servant and it was discovered my real talent lay as a comedic foil. A potentially life-changing revelation that I perhaps should have paid more attention to.

Moving the Hat

My best classes at U of D, besides those in the theater, were in philosophy—I don't remember one English class there, which isn't surprising because half the books I wanted to read were forbidden without special dispensation, how silly. My philosophy professor was a world-famous Thomistic scholar, and once he learned that I had spent a year with the Benedictines—the keepers of Thomistic philosophy as well as of the sacred chants— I was golden. I had him for several classes over the year I was at the university, and got to know him fairly well. One afternoon at the supermarket I ran into him trying to get through the check-out line while keeping track of his three toddlers. A distinguished man in his early fifties, he looked at me and said, "This is more difficult than the plurality of forms."

Since leaving St. Vincent I had discovered Existentialism and spent hours reading Sartre and Camus, and in my new role as a Catholic intellectual, worked to come up with a Catholic existentialism. When I thought I had solved the problem, I presented it to my professor. We met in the school cafeteria and, armed with a hundred-page-manuscript, carefully laid out my proposition. He listened attentively, nodding here and there, and when I was through, said, "Very impressive. Very well thought out."

"But do you think the argument holds up?"

He took a sip of coffee and looked at me kindly. "What I've found is that one can reason to any conclusion one wants. The truth is, I don't read philosophy anymore. I only read poetry." He held up a thin volume. "I particularly like Rimbaud, the French symbolists, you know?"

Even before that gut-punch my faith had been on shaky ground. I found the Jesuits to be brilliant, of course, but devoted to their purpose of using the intellect and all worldly means to further their agenda, no matter who they stepped on. The embodiment of the end justifies the means. A valid argument, but one I found I couldn't go along with when it meant having to ask permission, child-like, when there was something I might need to learn or experience. That Easter vacation, I treated myself to reading Camus' *The Plague*. Afterward, I stood on the overpass watching the traffic speeding by beneath me on the John Lodge and realized I no longer believed.

Richard Snodgrass

Moving the Hat

The second summer I was in Detroit I hung out with a student of De's named Tony, a Greek who wrote amazing stories about his relationship with a young woman he referred to only as The Turk, keeping alive in his attempts to seduce her the age-old hatred of the Greeks for the Turks. The problem was, although the events of the stories were reprehensible, they were also well-written and, sad to say, interesting. Tony's father owned a large industrial construction firm employing illegal Greek immigrants; several times Tony had me accompany him on a run across the bridge to Windsor, Ontario, where he parked on a back street, opened the trunk, and a couple of workers popped out, heading back home. Tony's family grew fond of me and ultimately gave me a peasant's house on Icaria; De once visited there but I never made it. Tony also asked me to marry his deflowered cousin, whose dowry was a house in Athens, a farm, and all the necessary servants, but I declined.

De introduced us both to a new faculty member, a novelist named Sam Astrachan. Sam was the darling of New York intellectuals after he published, right out of Columbia and with the imprimatur of his teacher, Lionel Trilling, a novel entitled *An End to Dying*. That summer Sam was teaching a creative writing class, and Tony and I both signed up. For my first story I wrote about a young janitor in a Catholic grade school who keeps crossing paths with a young sister in the big deserted building. Eventually, she trips over his bucket and runs to the chapel in hysterics, having a nervous breakdown, throwing herself onto the alter of the Lord, wracked with nameless guilts. When I read the story to the class, Sam looked at me for a moment, then announced, "Well, that's the way it's done. See you all next week." Afterwards the three of us went to a bar in Greektown, eating feta cheese sandwiches and drinking ouzo, where Sam told me that my story was the best student work he had ever encountered. "And if you write three or four hours every day for the next twenty years, you might accomplish something." Tony, hearing that, never wrote again. But I thought it sounded like a good deal and started my daily writing routine, which still holds true.

Moving the Hat

During the year-and-a-half I was in Detroit, every couple of weeks I would make the pilgrimage by bus to De and Jan's in Dearborn for the weekend. This was the time after winning the Pulitzer and his life was changing rapidly; he was traveling a lot on the poetry circuit giving readings across the country. His image was changing as well. He let his hair and beard grow and bought a knee-length greatcoat with a fur collar and a matching fur hat; he was beginning to look like an orthodox priest. Though his appearance seemed the least of his changes. On his travels to various colleges and universities he encountered poetry groupies, young women, and some not so young, students and professors and housewives who were attracted to poets, who attended his readings and offered themselves to him. Late at night De and I would go for coffee at a diner on Michigan Avenue a few blocks from his house and he would relate his latest adventures, the women he had slept with, as well as sometimes write out on a napkin a poem he was working on.

    The women were plentiful and attentive, which was not helping his already strained marriage to Jan. Closer to home he began an affair with a woman named Tibby whom he met in one of his night school classes. As he described it, he at first totally overlooked the plain almost mousy woman in his class, then one evening this gorgeous model dressed to the nines was sitting in that woman's seat: it turned out that Tibby was a model and for once had come straight from a photo shoot. Their affair started that night and continued on a regular basis, meeting at a local motel where they occupied themselves between bouts of the obvious with sitting on the bed trying to write a play together about a modeling agency. After several months, unable to keep away from her, De invited Tibby and her husband to the house for dinner—a desperate and ill-advised move that ended with me sitting with De afterward at a picnic table in the park across the street, their Great Dane, Ham, running freely over the grassy fields, as De slammed his fists down on the tabletop sobbing, "It's not fair, it's not fair, that that beautiful, intelligent, sexy woman and she's not with me!"

Already a mile above you;
~~a mile and miles away;~~
I don't know whether I love you
Or what I need to say.

Somewhere in all that city
You toss in your own bed
alone,—and moves the pity.
It's 80. below outside

And the world is far more distant
Than anyone ~~would~~ have ~~I~~ thought.
We touched, just for an ~~~~ instant
~~and were loving, or will not~~

~~A gust of desire~~ ~~~~ ~~awaken~~
~~Or hungers ~~~~ ~~~~ believe
~~~~ ~~~~ There's little else endures;

And who knows where this may finish
Or ~~if~~ how our loves might cross.
Let no loose word diminish
The blessedness or the loss.

As lust moved us ~~to despair~~
~~Or the~~ hunger as love cures
We wakened in each other. I swear
There's little else endures

Moving the Hat

When I was a teenager, De taught me about the dangers of love, about the deadliness of other's emotional tricks, the quicksand of settling for the easy way out. During my time in Detroit he impressed upon me that we have to take responsibility for every aspect of our lives, that there are winners and losers in this world and we have the ability and the power to determine which we are. And that the choice is actually a matter of life or death. In interviews he often cited Simone Weil as a major influence on his thinking, but he told me that a more direct influence, in addition to his on-going psychoanalysis, came from a book by Arnold A. Hutchsnecker, *The Will to Live*:

> *Thus it was in his later years, when genius had been mellowed by wisdom and experience, that Freud came to the culmination of his researches with his theory that two dynamic principles, one creative and the other destructive, are the basic forces from which all other instincts emanate.*
>
> *. . . Whether we call them instincts or responses, we are aware of these two opposing drives.*
>
> *How they function in each individual, in harmony or disharmony for health or sickness, for long life or early death, for the fullness of living or the poverty of I, depends upon the individual himself.*
>
> *There are those who believe that we determine not only our end but also the means by which we die. As Menninger stated it: 'In the end each man kills himself in his own selected way, fast or slow, soon or late.'*

To win in De's lexicon meant to make good on your desires, to realize what you want and pursue it with your whole being, your driving force; otherwise that energy will turn inward to destroy you—with an accident that was no accident at all, with a felling heart attack or stroke, with a cancer that eats you alive. De felt he was making good on his desires, his life force, by taking advantage of the women who were floating around him in those days; to refuse them would be to refuse life, to risk that sexual energy burrowing inward and destroying him. You certainly couldn't blame him for not wanting to hurt himself, could you?

Richard Snodgrass

Moving the Hat

But then he had been saying much the same to me, in one way or another, from the beginning. This from a letter written in the spring of 1958:

> P.P.S.
>
> I say this in all seriousness. This is a matter of the greatest importance. You are fighting for your soul, for your right to a future -- it is possible that you are literally fighting for your life. See that you are not distracted and see that you win.
>
> We're with you
>
> De

Talking with De wasn't always enjoyable, at times it was more like an emotional enema, but I'll say this, it was never dull.

Richard Snodgrass

Moving the Hat

After a few months at the University of Detroit, I could tell that the Jesuits and I weren't made for each other. Grades weren't the problem. At St. Vincent I realized I needed to make up for my high school career spent mainly in driving my family's hot red Oldsmobile up and down Seventh Avenue, and had taught myself to study—found I actually liked it and was good at it—and had been a straight-A, Dean's List student ever since. That Christmas De and Jan hosted a bunch of their literary friends for the holidays, including the Elliotts: George, an English professor and writer, and Mary Emma, an editor at the Hudson Review. At De's suggestion I told George I wanted to change schools and asked where the best English departments were. George said there were three: Harvard, but I didn't have the background; Yale, but I didn't have the money; which left the University of California, Berkeley. In fact, he was going to be teaching at Berkeley himself the following year, and encouraged me to apply.

I had never heard of Berkeley—the year was 1960—nor had I ever considered going to California, much less San Francisco and the Bay Area, but apply I did. In case I didn't make it, I also applied to Columbia, American University in D.C. (hesitant to give up the Catholic idea), Washington University in St. Louis, and a few others, making tours of the different schools and cities. But when I got the letter of acceptance to Berkeley, there was no question. The clincher was a book I came across on the remaindered table at a bookstore a few blocks from the U of D campus. Entitled, *New Images of Man*, it was the catalog of a recent exhibition at the Modern Museum of Art. From my travels to various schools and cities—I had begun my lifelong haunting of museums—I was acquainted with a number of the artists included, Bacon and Giacometti, de Kooning and Pollock, but there were two painters new to me, Nathan Oliveira and Richard Diebenkorn, both who totally laid me out. Their write-ups said they each worked in the San Francisco area and were part of what was called the Bay Area Figurative Movement. I decided I very much wanted to be in a place where such things were happening.

Richard Snodgrass

Moving the Hat

Strange to say, I had no preconceived notions of San Francisco, no notions of it at all, nor was I one who had spent their lives dreaming of sunny California where everything would be better, cars, girls, love. My only impression of San Francisco came from the old 1950s black and white TV police drama, *The Lineup*, with its b-roll of the hills and docks and bridges; later in life I rented an apartment on Russian Hill close to where behind the opening credits an unmarked police car comes up Hyde and turns in front of the camera to head down steep Lombard. When I decided I was definitely going to Berkeley, I picked up Jerry Stoller's book, *I Am a Lover*, with its grainy photographs of the city and North Beach, but I still had no particular expectations.

Then one morning I got on a plane and five hours later landed in a whole new world. A blue-and-white world, a white city on its seven hills, and when the August fogs came through the Golden Gate in the afternoons, an off-white world. Misty. Shades of light gray. Silvery at times. Ethereal. Not at all the sooty gray of the mill town where I was raised, where too often all colors were only shades of gray, red-gray, blue-gray, green-gray. I spent the first few days checked into a hotel on 5th Street a half a block below Market Street, and walked. Walked everywhere, the downtown, North Beach, Chinatown, Fisherman's Wharf, Russian Hill, Telegraph Hill, Nob Hill, discovering restaurants and bars I still frequented twenty years later, Tadich Grill, Columbus Hotel, Sears Fine Food, The Gold Spike, Tosca. Though with the sudden leap across the country it was months before I lost the sensation that Detroit and Pittsburgh, the world I knew previously, was just on the other side of the Berkeley Hills. It seemed I wasn't the only one who had trouble adjusting to my departure. Tony wrote to say that after they saw me off at the airport—Jan said she couldn't stand the goodbye—De, who was driving as they left the airport, suddenly veered off the road and stopped, got out and began wandering aimlessly along the shoulder, muttering to himself. Tony had to grab him and get him back in the car before he got run over and ended up the one who drove them back to Dearborn.

Richard Snodgrass

Moving the Hat

In the early Sixties, there were as many students at UC Berkeley as there were people in my hometown of Beaver Falls, 20,000+; when protests against the university started shortly after I arrived—there was no connection—the protesters handed out IBM punch cards with the words Free Speech spelled by the holes, and the message was well taken. To keep track of that many students required a machine-like efficiency, but I found the anonymity to my liking, and I could go on about my business without being noticed. My business being first of all to play catchup with thousands of students who were infinitely better prepared academically than I was.

My first semester I had Josephine Miles' class on the lyric, which required an essay comparing two poets each week; Ian Watts' class on critical writing, another essay a week; Henry Nash Smith's survey of American literature, which required a well-researched thesis; a required Spanish class that I was able to squeak through because of the young woman graduate assistant who took pity on my faltering attempts to translate Neruda. I was only able to ace a required physics course because of my bony knees: the class was held in a steep European-style theater, and on test days I found if I placed my knee just so the girl in front of me, a cute Cal Cheerleader—Go Bears!—had to tilt her head to the side, leaving her test paper spread before me. I've never been one to solve my problems by cheating, that wasn't the way I was raised, and I certainly wasn't proud of it; though that grade was obtained surreptitiously—I knew there was no way I could pass with my mathematically-deficient brain—I had the satisfaction of knowing I had more than earned my grades in all my other classes. Still, I was amazed at the end of the semester to find I had once again made the Dean's List. L'il ol' me: on the Dean's List at Berkeley! The upshot was, however, that having found I could hold my own with the best students at one of the best schools in the world, I more or less packed it in and floated through my remaining semesters, content with passing grades, taking what I found useful from the classes, and only playing the student-game otherwise to get passing grades.

Richard Snodgrass

Moving the Hat

After the first semester at Berkeley when I established my academic credentials to myself, my life became something of a balancing act between attending classes and taking care of all my other activities. A standing tenet of the intellectual culture of the 1950s, '60s, and '70s was that entering into psychotherapy—or even better, psychoanalysis—gave you credibility as an intellectual and a worthwhile individual, someone who was seeking the roots of their darkest desires and therefore could be respected in their insights and motivations. Now, if you've followed this narrative this far, you've noticed that I could certainly have used some therapy at one point or another, if only to deal with my brother's free-wheeling do-it-yourself one-size-fits-all home-grown Freudianism. But like so many of my generation I considered therapy a rite of passage, something I needed to go through in order to achieve true maturity. So, within a few months I entered into a program at the University Health Services—wow, talk about cred: therapy at the University of California! I must really have problems and be an interesting person!

My brother's emphasis on freeing myself from dependance on our parents was still very much in play, so I took a part-time job as janitor of a sporting goods store in Oakland, 35-hours a week sweeping and waxing floors, emptying wastepaper baskets, being the lookout while the owner entertained his ladylove among the lawn furniture on the third floor. I had found a cottage for myself in a back yard a mile or so from campus, and to get back and forth between school and job I bought (ahem, with my parents' help; the doctrine wasn't flawless) a used Vespa motor scooter, zipping along the streets day and night. A surprise came when I applied for my senior year and was informed because of my work hours I was considered a resident of the state, reducing my tuition from $300 a year to zero, with only an $84 incidental fee. My father, who was prepared to shell out thousands of dollars to a major university like the rest of his business associates, and who had had trouble accepting the first year that tuition was only $300, was incensed when I told him there was no tuition at all, it convinced him that the education must be worthless. Poor Father. I didn't tell him that I picked up the $84 fee on my own.

Richard Snodgrass

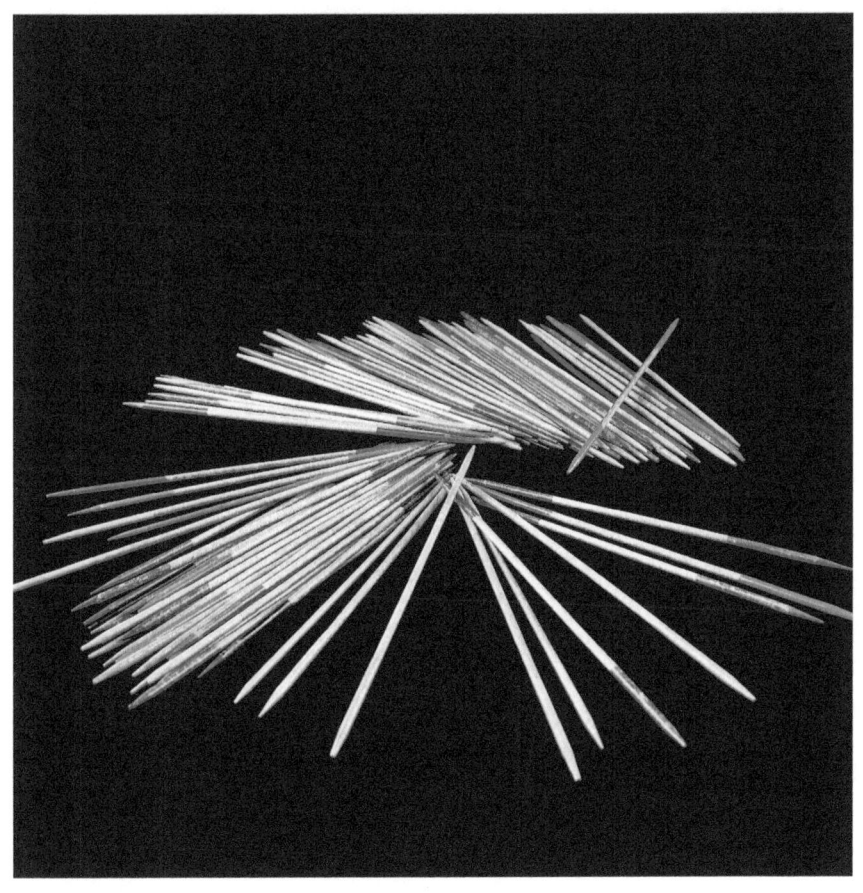

Moving the Hat

When I moved to California, a part of me hoped to leave my brother behind, though as life would have it, another part of me apparently packed him away tidily in a corner of my suitcase, along with all those other things that take up the least amount of space when you're relocating but end up making the new place very much the same as the place you left. It didn't take long for the Berkeley English Department to discover they had the brother of the Pulitzer Prize winner—oh, *that* Snodgrass—in their midst. Nor did it help when one day in Josephine Miles' class one of the stars of the department, a graduate student who had a perpetual chip on his shoulder, said in a discussion on contemporary poetry that he considered W. D. Snodgrass a "kitchen poet." Miss Miles, who knew my background from George Elliott, smiled and said, "Well, let's ask another Snodgrass what he thinks of that statement." All eyes turned to me. But for once I delivered a comeback that I'm proud of to this day: "I think W. D. would say he thought kitchens were very important."

Toward the end of my second semester the department hosted De for a reading and a number of appearances while he was in town for the San Francisco Poetry Festival. For a couple of days we had great fun as I ferried him around perched on the back of my Vespa between student receptions and faculty teas, delivering him at one point through Ian Watt's garden. At the festival I witnessed the famous poet in action, with admirers, sycophants, and interested women surrounding him everywhere he went. De loved it. When I got lost as to where I fit in with all this, one of De's fellow poets from Iowa, Philip Levine, came to my rescue and got me seated; he said he understood my predicament, his own brother had explained to him the difficulties of being the brother of the poet. Afterward at a reception at Enrico's, De pulled me aside, dug a half a dozen hotel room keys from his coat pocket, and explained which key belonged to which girl. "Take your pick, I'm sure they'd settle for the brother." I declined, but not on moral grounds, sad to say; I wasn't experienced at that time and was afraid I'd embarrass myself.

Richard Snodgrass

Moving the Hat

George Elliott joined the faculty at Berkeley in my second semester, and I visited George and Mary Emma's house in the Berkeley Hills once or twice a week for a meal or just talk. They often hosted visiting writers and they invited me to all their soirees; during the Cuban Missile Crisis we sat at their dining room table looking out the picture window at San Franciso across the Bay, expecting to see it dissolve in a mushroom cloud at any second. I took all of George's creative writing classes, but I was never much good. George believed you couldn't teach vision, but you could teach revision, and he revised the life right out of things. De said George was his literary conscience, and had gone out of his way to praise George's recent book-length poem, *Fever and Chills*, as the harbinger of a new direction in American poetry. It wasn't, but it was nice of De to say so.

Feelings were often strained between them, mainly from George's disapproval of De's reaction to his growing fame—and I suspect from George's lack of same. One early rift came when they both read at the San Francisco Poetry Festival, where De was lauded and George was not. Apparently after the reading George drove us somewhere and hit a bump pretty hard. De commented on it in letter dated July 8, 1962:

> *...I guess I didn't get an award for reading at the Festival. (That incidentally is why George jolted us over that bump – he was mad because when I came in the house I said "They're giving awards at the festival for reading! Maybe I'll get an extra $25.00! Whee!" He says in the good old pre-Pulitzer day I'd have remembered he read there and would of said, "Maybe we'll get an . . . . " And he takes that as proof of my corruption! All right it was tactless – but I was thinking of that theorbo and whether or not I could afford it. . . . . did it seem that bad to you? Oh well . . . .*

Over the years as the rift grew, I was a kind of balancing point between them, conveying messages and explaining what the other must have meant when such-and-such was said or done. In time that rift grew into a three-way crevice so wide and deep that it swallowed us all.

Richard Snodgrass

July 8? 1965
Sunday anyway,

Dear Dick,

If you think things seem dull + depressing since I left there, you should try them HERE!!! I've been having great bouts of concience, terrors of **V.D.**, expectations of cosmic retribution, and just about the time I had things sortof—maybe under control, I get a letter from George full of comments on corruption and how he can give up fame after seeing what it's done to me! My instruments still haven't arrived -- when they come, I'll simply cut my throat and have done with it!

And yet, you know, it WAS good to have lived -- if only for a week. It was so fine to feel alive for a change! And by God, I did feel alive there! I wonder if I'll ever feel that way again? By the way, I thought you'd be interested to hear that I didn't have to take a bus to the airport -- it seems that a red MG came to the door, see, and this girl with the long blonde hair.... well, Jesus Christ! (I'm glad I wrote this -- I'm beginning to come to life again!) Came by to see what I was doing that evening ...... flopped onto the bed on top of me.... Jesus God, did any of these things happen?

Good Lord, I love corruption!
I shall be voted Most Corruptible.

Moving the Hat

"This balance thing," Marty says. "How long has that been going on?"

"It's like I said before. Scientists say from the beginning of time, maybe it was the beginning of time itself or the universe or reality. . .or whatever. There's always been this counteraction between plus and minus, positive and negative energy, the zero electrical charge. . . ."

Marty is shaking her head. "No, I mean with you personally. How long have you been aware of the importance of balance?"

"Since I lost mine." I think it's a clever answer but Marty just looks at me. "Only recently. I was never aware of the idea of balance as a unifying concept until I started putting these snippets and images together." Then my cleverness gets the better of me. "But when I was a kid I wanted to be a tightrope walker. Does that count?"

Marty is looking dubiouser and dubiouser.

"My family always went to the big circus shows when they came to Pittsburgh, and one of the main attractions of those shows was a high-wire act called The Flying Wallenda's. They were famous for working without a net, and they would build a pyramid three and four levels high with people standing on other people's shoulders, somebody all the way on top, and they would come walking out across the wire. Everybody would be gasping and holding their breath, scared to death, though my Uncle Stu was never impressed, he'd just sit there as blasé as could be. "Doesn't bother me a bit," he'd say. "I just don't believe it's happening."

"And you wanted to be a Wallenda?"

"Yeah, I got this idea I had really good balance. Remember, we're talking about a chubby eight-year-old kid here who couldn't even do a somersault. I'd lay a length of clothesline on the floor in the hall between the living room and dining room and walk along it with my arms outstretched like it was a high wire. TaDa! The Great Snodgrassa! Then one day my sainted sisters tried to help by tying the line between our two sycamores in the backyard, but it was only six inches off the ground and they could never get it tight enough. Just as well. Every time I tried to step on it I'd tumble off. Another dream of glory shot to hell. You don't mess around with real."

Moving the Hat

I spent my last semester at Cal, instead of studying for Finals, hitchhiking around the Northwest, most of the time camped out in a virgin forest beside a lake on Vancouver Island reading Gary Snyder, Blyth's haiku translations, and Haida myths. While passing through the university district in Seattle, in a mostly deserted coffeehouse, I met a folk singer named Roger Perkins from San Francisco, a tall red-haired, red-bearded fellow my age; when I told him I was from Berkeley he greeted me like we had known each other in a past life. From the first he struck me as the gentlest, meekest person I ever encountered. As we spent the afternoon talking between his sets, he said that he and his friends were living in an abandoned mansion in Pacific Heights and that I should look him up when I got back.

The house was on Broadway, a few blocks from the tunnel into North Beach, a three-story Victorian slated to be leveled for a new motel-style apartment building. When I rang the bell and told the girl who answered about meeting Roger in Seattle, she welcomed me like a long-lost member of the tribe. Soon I was sitting on a mattress on the floor of what had once been the living room, drinking Red Mountain Burgundy and smoking weed and meeting the others who lived there. It seemed everyone had come to the house from meeting Roger some place or other, at one of his gigs, a friend of a friend, or just passing on the street, everyone taken by his gentleness, almost saintliness. There were a dozen people or so, most of them folk singers of one ilk or another, though there were others, a student teacher, a former Green Beret, a nurse's aide. Roger was a guitar guru, known for his finger-picking style taken from Elizabeth Cotton; he also sometimes accompanied a Texas folk singer named Janis Joplin, who bopped in and out to either rehearse or to screw him, no matter his live-in girlfriend. When night came, Roger fixed me up in the room of his singing partner, Larry Hanks, who was gone for the day, each member of the house coming in to wish me good-night, good-night. In the morning, though, Roger sent around a cowboy singer named Cal Robertson to tell me Larry was due back later and that I had to leave. Sorry, pardner, now saddle up, vamoose.

Moving the Hat

My misstep—I'm reluctant to call it a mistake, but it probably was—was forcing myself into a situation where I didn't belong, where I didn't fit in, where, truth be told, I wasn't particularly wanted. For the next few weeks I hung out at the house, getting to know everyone who lived there, telling myself I was one of them, hoping a room might open up so I could move in. And it was interesting, something was always going on, music filled the house, I was living the folk music scene. When no rooms opened up after a couple of weeks, one day Cal said, "Well, there's always that empty storage room in the basement." He meant it as a sarcastic joke, some brand of cowboy humor, but I went down and looked at it, and paid the going rate to Fat Sally who collected rents for the realtor. She said I was nuts but was happy enough to take my money. It was a small room, maybe 10 by 16, the ceiling only a foot above my head, the only window looking out at eye-level to the walk between the houses, on a concrete ledge beside a space for a car. I hung decorator fishnet from the ceiling for a touch of atmosphere, picked up a mattress at Good Will, ran an extension cord from the electrical box for a lamp and hotplate, and moved in with my suitcases and boxes of books. I spent the days listening to the sounds of footsteps overhead, music filtering down the cellar stairs, sitting on my mattress reading Kenneth Patchen and Robinson Jeffers, writing bad short stories and worse poems and feeling very with it.

In time I attained a grudging acceptance as a member of the house, aided no doubt by the fact I had a car, a VW Beetle named Oliver BIP my folks got me as a graduation present; most evenings were taken up ferrying somebody to their gig at a bar or coffeehouse, my payment sitting beside the stage as a makeshift roadie. I got to hear a lot of music that way, and knew the ins and outs of the setups. For a while Roger and Larry and I tried to form a trio, with me playing my dumbeck to their guitar and recorder noodling, some sort of hybrid melting of Appalachia meets Morocco, but it never came off.

Richard Snodgrass

Moving the Hat

The house came to an abrupt end the morning the realtor showed up and we found out he had no idea we were living there; Fat Sally only said she made the arrangements and pocketed the rent money for herself. Graciously, the realtor gave us three days to clear out before he came back with the Sheriff. Roger and Larry asked me to join them in getting an apartment—let's be realistic: including me would lower their rent and there was the matter of the car. But no matter, I belonged. A mutual acquaintance told us of a really cool undiscovered area of town, mainly White Russian, with old Victorian houses and dirt-cheap rents, a delicatessen that stocked Guinness Stout and Rainier Ale, and a restaurant called the Good Eats that served a killer chicken Kiev for $7.00. The area went by the name Haight-Ashbury.

We found a flat at the rear of a house on Page Street and divided the three rooms between us. The problem was that to get to the kitchen you had to go through either my or Larry's room; I said I needed my privacy to write—the first strike against me—so Larry's room also served as a corridor, not to his liking. The flat quickly became a meeting place for Larry and Roger's girlfriends and groupies, as well as panhandlers, down-and-outers, runaways, druggies and anyone else who gentle Roger invited home. The nights fell into a pattern: everyone gathered in Larry's room for cheap wine, weed, LSD, peyote buttons, and whatever else was currently making the rounds. Strike two: after hallucinating wildly one night on grass, I took to staying in my room. I had several run-ins with Roger's houseguests when I came home and found somebody rummaging through my clothes or books. Roger only ducked his head, looked little-boyish, and said, "People got to do what they got to do." Strike three came when I woke one night, smelled something burning, went to the kitchen and found a stranger sitting with his street-blackened feet propped up on the kitchen table, cooking down heroin in my saucepan. "Hey man, you want some of this?" I picked him up and threw him, literally, down the back stairs. Fortunately he was so high the two-story tumble didn't faze him. It was agreed, however, that it would be best if I got a place of my own.

Richard Snodgrass

Moving the Hat

It was a four-story mustard-colored Victorian, complete with tower and dormered windows on a mansard roof—a mansion at one time, before it was cut up into apartments—on the corner of Shrader and Oak Streets a block from Golden Gate Park. My first apartment in the building was on the third floor, basically a one-room affair tucked in between two lightwells, with a squished bathroom, galley-style kitchen, and a murphy bed: after the hippies I was never so happy to be alone in my life. When the elderly woman across the hall was found dead—I wondered about the smell—I moved into her place after it was aired out. Two generous-sized rooms, a full bathroom, a genuine kitchen, a bay window looking down at the traffic streaming along the Panhandle toward the downtown. Heaven. For the first time since I left Berkeley I had a table to do my four-hours-a-day writing. I bought new pots and pans including a Dutch oven that I called my first appliance. I learned to cook beef stew from a recipe in the *Chronicle* that would last me a week at a time. I only had a mattress on the floor but I bought a nice coverlet for it. I built bookshelves out of the crates with beautiful dovetail corners found at night on the curbs in Chinatown. For the first time I felt I was making inroads on being an adult.

And I learned the ins-and-outs of sex. I had had a few experiences by this time, all bad enough to make me hesitant to try again. But one day I got to talking to a young woman named Susannah who lived at the end of the hall; in the course of conversation and trying to figure out whether we wanted to date or not, we admitted to each other that we didn't know the first thing about how to do sex. Accordingly, that Saturday we launched into a program of experimenting with every position, technique, act, whatever we had ever heard of, practicing through the weekend until we felt we got them right. I certainly felt accomplished. Afterward, we decide that with all that we really didn't want to see each other again, but a week later she left a package at my door, a sterling silver belt buckle engraved with an inscription from Grimm's Tale of "The Little Tailor":

SEVEN WITH ONE BLOW

Richard Snodgrass

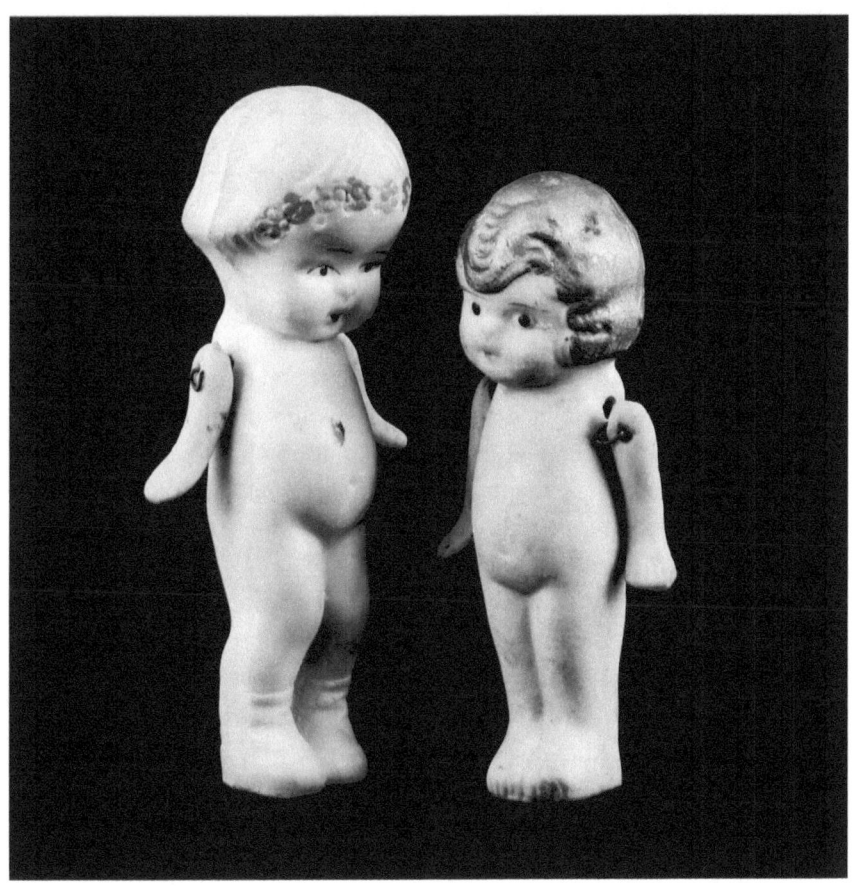

Moving the Hat

One of the advantages, and maybe disadvantages, of being at Berkeley in the early Sixties was the easy access to news of current events outside of mainstream media. Which meant we were quite aware of a war going on in some faraway land called Vietnam long before the majority of Americans. At the same time I became aware that my student deferment would end when I graduated. I don't know how I would have reacted, say, in World War II or Korea where our cause was just. But this war? We learned from alternate news sources that everything about this "police action" was simply wrong, even immoral. I could have gone to graduate school to avoid the draft, but I chose to be a conscientious objector.

I certainly had the religious background for it. So I started the long administrative journey of obtaining C. O. status, offering to do five or even ten years alternate service as a civilian nurse's aide. The procedure meant many levels of applications, interviews, more applications; eventually I was the subject of an FBI investigation that lasted more than six months. At one point I had to travel back to Beaver Falls for a hearing with my local draft board; De volunteered as a character witness but he ended up lecturing these small-town folks on principles of Good and Evil. They made it clear they did not appreciate being preached to by a famous poet who they remembered as a precocious teenager.

Through it all my Quaker councilor helped me manage the red tape. He also tried to impress upon me what awaited a nice White college boy when I was sent to Federal prison at Leavenworth; though I said I understood what to expect, my convictions overshadowed any threat. Foolish me. Knowing then what I know now of all the goes on in prisons, I'm not sure I would have gone through with it. But at the time: Onward Christian Soldiers, even if my claim was based more on Buddhism.

Richard Snodgrass

Moving the Hat

And then, after all the rigamarole, the government decided it didn't want me anyway.

I remember it was still dark the morning I drove to Oakland for my Army induction physical; there were rats in the gutters on Oak Street, their eyes glowing in my headlights and they would not scare. I thought it quite symbolic. I parked in a garage across the street from the Induction Center; I had given a set of keys to a friend, along with instructions about my apartment, fully expecting not to return. Because my status as a Conscientious Objector was still denied, I had no alternative except to refuse induction at the end of the physical. When told to take one step forward, legally making me part of the army, I would just stand there, waiting for the MPs to take me away.

I remember only snippets of that morning. I remember when I checked in a sergeant looked at my paperwork and said, "Oh, you're Snodgrass. Our Objector for the day." I remember standing around with a hundred other guys in our underwear. I remember peeing in a plastic cup, just to prove that I could in public. I remember line after line. "Cough. Again. Turn around, bend over, spread your cheeks." I remember becoming increasingly lightheaded, detached, at one point wanting to go over and crouch against the baseboard like a mouse. After taking my temperature and blood pressure, they sent me to see a doctor. A bear of a man, with a monk's tonsure, he looked at my chart, looked at me. "Have you been ill?" "No, sir." "Are you aware that your temperature is 104 and your blood pressure is 205 over 100?" "No, sir." He looked at my file. "Conscientious Objector. The truth is you just don't want to go, do you, son?" "No sir, I don't." He shook his head. "I don't know why they put boys like you through this. You wouldn't make a good soldier, you'd question everything." He wrote in my file then threw it at me. "You're 4-F. Now get the hell out of here!" I remember I spent the rest of the day sitting on a slope in the Berkeley Hills with a view of San Francisco across the Bay, feeling like I had awakened from a long coma, having to relearn the world again, repeating to myself the names of things: Grass. Earth. Sky. Tree.

Moving the Hat

"Carlos Castenada talks about making a recapitulation of your life, remembering it segment by segment, reliving in your mind all the important people and places you've known, not to criticize or find fault, but to understand the things that make up your life so far. He thought it was the most effective way to sever your connections with the past. So you could be truly free to experience the present."

Marty is busy folding her underwear after I bring up the clothes from doing the laundry. "And is that what you're doing with these snippets? Making a recapitulation?"

"It didn't start out to be. But it's beginning to look that way."

"I thought they came to the conclusion ol' Carlos was a fraud."

"True. They found out all the teachings of Don Juan, the supposed Yaqui sorcerer, could be found in books Castaneda had access to in the UCLA library, but—"

"Doesn't that put the kibosh on the whole thing?" Marty holds up a pair of her panties, exams them for something, then peeks around them at me.

"George Elliott once said that either Castaneda was the greatest anthropologist of our time, or the greatest novelist. And that it really didn't matter which, the things Castaneda said were critical."

"From what you've noted so far, I'm not sure I'd take a recommendation from George Elliott as the final word."

"There were times when Castaneda's ideas, wherever they came from, were really important to me, they got me through some bad times in San Francisco. And they helped me get beyond all the ideas De laid on me. And I think Castaneda helped me to laugh more."

"You do laugh a lot. Thank heavens." Marty makes a pair of her panties do a little dance. I laugh.

"It's what he called Controlled Folly. Acting as if what you do is important when you know it isn't. Taking what you do seriously without taking yourself seriously. Something I've tried to live by. For years I carried a three-by-five card to remind me of the ideas I wanted to follow."

"That's really sweet in a way. Earlier you were talking about the sayings your father used to live by. Like father, like son."

"I don't know if that's a good thing or bad."

"Maybe it just is."

Richard Snodgrass

Choose your own battlefields.

Discard everything that is not essential.

Put your life on the line.
   Any battle is the battle for one's life.

Relax, abandon yourself, fear nothing.
   Only then will the powers that guide us
   open the road and aid us. Only then.

When the odds are too great, retreat, regroup.

Compress time, every second counts.
   In the battle for your life,
   a second is an eternity.

Never push yourself to the front.

Moving the Hat

After I graduated, I worked several jobs, each stranger than the last. First I was the janitor in a medical building in Berkeley. There were eight psychiatrists, each doctor with very specific requirements on how their office was to be cleaned. For instance, one wanted the tracks of the vacuum cleaner to be vertical, another wanted them horizontal, all to be lined up as precisely as corn rows. Speaking of neurotic behavior. When I moved to San Francisco I was the fourth person in a four-person company—there were two bosses, a secretary, and me—that produced a knock-off of the Kelley Blue Book, the bible of used car prices. My job varied from warehouseman, depreciation calculator, address-o-graph operator, mailroom clerk. Later I moved on to a company that monitored news broadcasts. I sat before a bank of typewriters, television sets, and tape recorders attached to radios, and made one-sentence summaries of all the morning news stories. All was fine until one morning footage popped up on all the screens of a Vietnamese monk sitting calmly in flames after setting himself on fire. I got up and left and never went back.

With no possibility that I might be drafted, I put on my ill-fitting, out-of-fashion, charcoal gray high school graduation suit and set out to find a real job. I made the rounds of all the downtown employment agencies and was sent on an endless array of interviews for management training programs for hotels, resorts, airlines, financial services. From only a phone interview with the Royal Bank of Scotland I was practically guaranteed a position—A Berkeley graduate with the veddy British name of Snodgrass: the manager spoke like I was the answer to a dream. My interview there was the next morning, but in one those mysterious, serendipitous, life-changing moments, I decided to check out one more agency. I found it tucked away down a narrow corridor at the back of a pre-earthquake building off Market Street. Sitting at a bare desk in an otherwise empty one-room office was a middle-aged, overdone woman named Mrs. Bauman. She glanced at my resume, talked to me for fifteen minutes or so, and then announced: "Things, Richard. All these jobs you've interviewed for have you dealing with people. All very glamorous, dear, but it's obvious you don't really like people all that much. You need to work with things, Richard. Things."

Richard Snodgrass

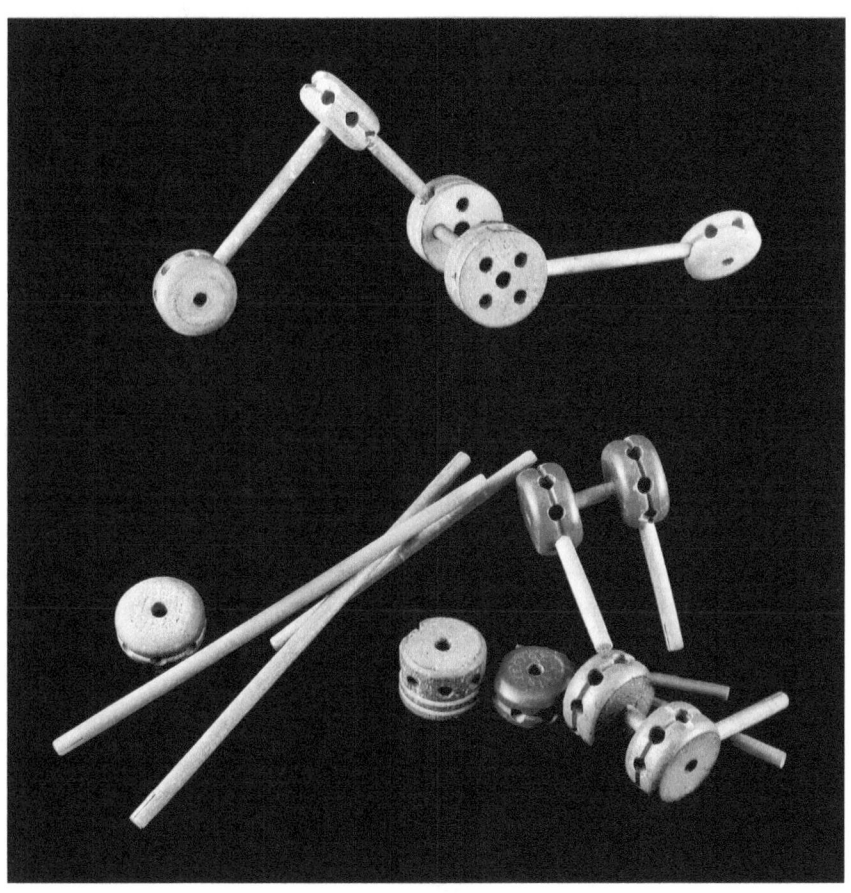

Moving the Hat

The job with "things" Mrs. Bauman sent me on was for a concrete inspector on a high-rise building under construction in the Financial District. I couldn't imagine me a construction worker, so just in case, I wore my suit minus the jacket under my scruffy clothes, thinking I could always change in my car for the Royal Bank of Scotland interview. It was the 43-story Wells Fargo Building at Sutter and Montgomery, soon to be the tallest building in the city though it was only up to 22-stories now. The inspection office was in a nearby building along with the steel erectors, sullen ironworkers clanking in and out. The chief inspector, Rick Ritchie, was busy but he gave me a hard hat and sent me down to find Walter, the concrete inspector who was with the trucks unloading inside the fence. Walter was a slim man in his early forties who looked like Bugs Bunny, complete to the buck teeth and bulbous-toed work boots, though without the ears. He was also obviously gay. When I told him who I was he took me by the arm and led me away from the noise, asking me, "Do you like to cook?" "Well, yes." "So you're comfortable with recipes." "Yes. . . ." "Wonderful! Because that's all concrete is, a recipe. We're going to have lot's of fun. Tell Rickie you're okay by me."

Back in the inspection office, things had quieted down; Rickie Ritchie was sitting with his feet up on the desk reading the *Chronicle*. He was in his early fifties, a Scot with a thick brogue who looked like a shorter version of Prince Phillip, wearing a herringbone tweed jacket, polo shirt, and pointy-toed dress shoes. After asking about Walter, he unrolled some blueprints and had me identify certain elements; I had mechanical drawing in high school, and was surprised how quickly I remembered how to read drawings. Then he handed me the building specifications, pointed to a passage, and asked me to explain it in simple terms. An English major, I was trained to interpret texts, so again, no problem. "Is that what that says?" Scotty Ritchie made a face. "I always wondered, never could make head nor tail of it." Then he looked at me suspiciously . "Snodgrass. T'is an English name." "No, Scottish." "T'is no. Whereabouts?" "Lowlands. Ayrshire." He exploded in glee. "Och! My folks are from Ayrshire! You've got the job!"

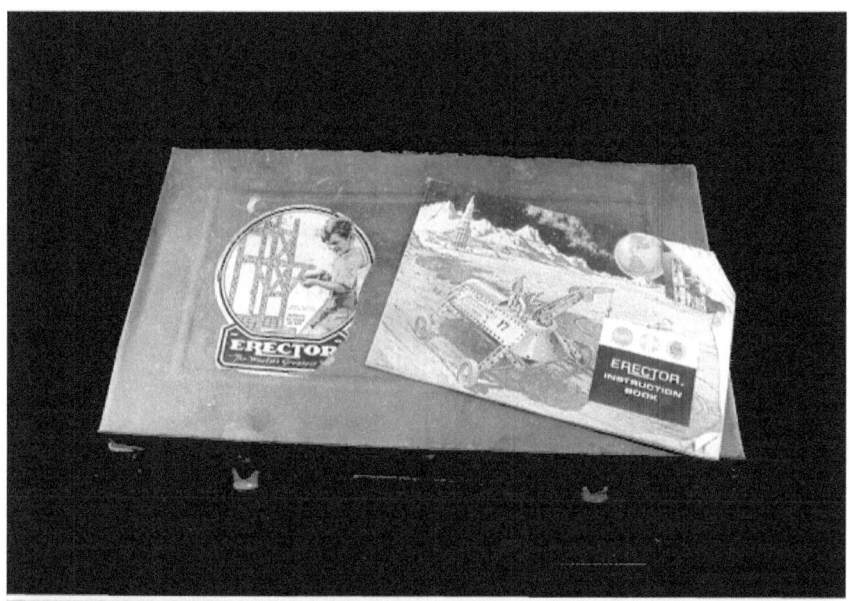
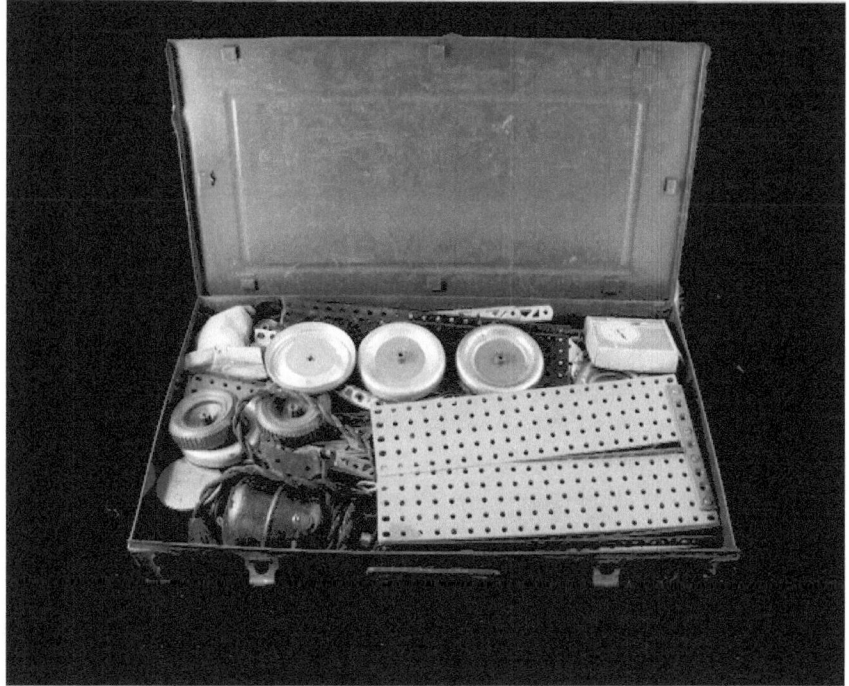

Moving the Hat

Over the next few days under Walter's tutelage, I learned that inspecting concrete meant devotion to a mystical quality of wet concrete known as Slump. It was the subject of endless conversations: "What's the Slump of that concrete?" "Add any more water and you'll ruin the Slump." "I can't pour concrete with a Slump like that." It seems that concrete, this mixture of cement, water, sand, and gravel, for all its hardness when fully set, is actually quite delicate in its formative stage. Not enough moisture and the concrete won't flow where it's supposed to go; too much moisture and the concrete won't reach the strength it's designed for. Slump was the way to measure the moisture of wet concrete. An experienced inspector could pretty much tell the Slump of a batch of concrete by watching it flow down the chute from the mixer, how it broke over the internal fins of the revolving drum. But there was an official test for Slump, appropriately called the Slump Test. It consisted of placing scoops of wet concrete in a foot-tall conical form, slowly lifting the form, and watching the concrete. . .er, Slump. Not enough water, the cone-shaped concrete stayed erect as it was; too much water and the concrete slid down into a puddle. There were other tests too, checking the temperature, the amount of air in the mix, taking sample cylinders to be tested in the lab. Otherwise my job was to watch the trucks unload the concrete into a hopper to be lifted to the floor being poured, occasionally climbing up on the back of the trucks as they arrived to eyeball the Slump inside the drum, a procedure that always reminded me of peering into the ass end of an elephant.

Scotty had me stay with the trucks for the first couple of weeks. But Scotty was a showman, and a showman needs an audience. As soon as the pour in the morning was going smoothly, Scotty had me accompany him as he walked the building—it was understood that I keep a respectful half-step behind—taking the man-hoist, the elevator on the outside of the building, up to the current top floor, then walking down, alternating stairwells to see the work underway on each floor as Scotty expounded on this and that, repeating the procedure in the afternoon. We soon became known as Scotty and Snotty.

Richard Snodgrass

It was a common joke on the building that the main reason I was hired was that I was the only one who could understand Rick's thick brogue or his Scottish sayings: "Aye, whit's fur ye'll no go by ye." "Ye ken I came up the Clyde in a tin bath?" Or as he told me once, "Your heid is filled with wee beasties. And they're all deid." He was a rogue, but a likeable one. Over time I pieced together that he started out as a grifter in Blackpool; at some time or other he was probably a welder in the Glascow shipyards, but an inspector? Not hardly. The thing was, he was never dull. One noontime a girl's pipe band from Vancouver paraded down Montgomery Street, advertising the Scottish games that weekend. As the band marched past, Scotty fell in behind, swinging his arms in that stiff-armed, fist-curled marching step of the British Army, calling to me over his shoulder, "Come on, lad, if ye want your job." I hurried to catch up and the two of us, in our hard hats, marched with them through the streets to Union Square.

I didn't learn a whole lot from Scotty about buildings or construction, he left that to the other inspectors (it may be that he didn't know that much himself about anything except welding steel), but I did learn you could make each day fun if you set your mind to it. He taught me to be delighted with the little things that happened in the everyday. To be playful. Unpredictable. Irreverent. I realize now he became the older brother I didn't know I was missing. Eventually he had me inspecting other areas—fireproofing, light welding, plastering. But most important of all he taught me I had to stand up for myself, something I was taught that nice people like us didn't do. A lesson I needed badly. One afternoon while walking the building by myself, a welder named Red Dog, a red-haired middle-aged man, stood up from where he was working, grabbed me by the arm, and spit into my face, "All your life you've got by by being a nice guy, haven't you? Smiling your way through life. Hey everybody, please like me. Well, that won't work out here. You've got to toughen up or these guys will eat you alive. It's more important in the world to be respected than liked. Now get the hell out of my sight."

Richard Snodgrass

Moving the Hat

My nemesis was the jobsite superintendent, a man named A. E. MacDonald known as Mac. He was an old man, nobody knew how old except he had been a superintendent on Grand Colee Dan, meaning he was in his sixties or seventies, his face an array of pouches and wrinkles. Mac was famous for his tirades, stringing together obscenities for minutes on end. "You goddamn motherfucking cocksucking pigsticking fatherdiddling lily-livered candy-ass son-of-a-bitching jacking-off know-nothing shit-eating ass-licking. . . ," you get the idea; I had witnessed strong men brought to tears under such rhythmic abuse. Just as bad though not as vocal was the general foreman, Jack Martin, a bully-faced pot-bellied guy whom the architect described as a tough Broderick Crawford. No question Jack was tough, he broke up fights by stepping between the guys and saying, "The two of you together can't take me so get back to work." So far I had avoided run-ins with either one but a couple times I came close enough to turn my bowels to water.

Scotty kept encouraging me to stand up to them, which is why I figure one day he sent me up to look at some rebar before a concrete pour. I had only been on the project a month and wasn't really sure what rebar was—reinforcing steel—but off I went to the fourth floor to inspect an elevated pad for a generator. It was simple enough on the drawings, #4's at 12 inches on center. Jack stood over me as I looked at it. "See? That's what I got. #4's at 12. So I can pour it, right?" He stuck his face in my face, but something wasn't right. Then I caught it. "What about the dowels for the block wall?" "Geesh, first he wants approved drawings, now he wants dowels, too." Then we both noticed the figure in khakis and old-style tin hat coming across the floor. "Uh oh," Jack said, "Good luck telling the Old Man why this isn't poured yet." Mac slouched up and started his tirade aimed at me: "No goddamn motherfucking cocksucking pigsticking fatherdiddling wet-behind-the-ears inspector is going to—" etcetera, etcetera. The Beatles were playing the Cow Palace that day, and it occurred to me, What would John Lennon do at a moment like this? I leaned close to the old man, smiled, and said, "Ah Mac, you look so cute when you get mad."

Richard Snodgrass

Moving the Hat

Time stopped. The universe gasped. Okay, those are exaggerations, but that end of the floor grew distinctly quiet as the Old Man stared at me. Then Jack, just back from pulling in some ironworkers to set the dowels, hollered, "Let's pour this sucker!" and the floor came to life again. Generators started up, the placing crew and finishers got busy, the laborers ran with their buggies to get the concrete from the hoist. Mac came to life too, starting in on a new tirade aimed at me but I walked away ignoring him, infuriating him even more. For a few minutes he followed me, shouting away as I circled the pad a couple of times, then I stopped abruptly, Mac almost running into me. I gave him another facetious smile, pumped my eyebrows a couple times, did a little John Lennon shuffle, and kept walking. Mac followed me a few steps then slouched off toward the manhoist. Across the pad Jack looked at me, puffed his lips, and flicked his cigarette into the wet concrete.

After the pour, I spent the afternoon walking the upper floors, keeping an eye out for either Mac or Jack, half expecting them to show up with a band of goons to beat the crap out of me. When it was quitting time I avoided the manhoist and walked down the stairs to the basement, figuring to take the shortcut between buildings through a service tunnel to our office. I was midway through the narrow passageway when I saw Jack coming toward me from the other direction. I thought I was a goner. He blocked my way, legs spread, feet planted, his ready-for-anything stance, beer belly swelling out of his open windbreaker, hands jammed deep in his baggy black jeans. And grinned. "That old man's a pistol, ain't he?" What? He leaned close, a friendly shark. "Did you really tell Old Mac he looked cute when he got mad? I was over with the rodbusters so I didn't hear. Wow, you got some cajónes on you. All the guys are talking about it, you're a local hero. Come on, I'll buy you a drink." Later I learned Mac was actually pleased I came back at him, he had been concerned I wasn't tough enough to make it on the jobsite. After that, Mac told Jack he was to give "the boy" anything I asked for, he said they needed a good inspector looking out for them.

Richard Snodgrass

Moving the Hat

Drinking with Jack after work became a regular occurrence. Mac requested me on a number of other projects over the next ten years, not because I was in his pocket but because he found he could trust me. "If the boy says it's so, it's so." He backed me without question the time I rejected thirteen floors of sprayed fireproofing—Mac told the subcontractor if he said one cross word to me the guy would never walk straight again—the time I rejected a dozen concrete trucks in a row. That I earned the respect of Mac and Jack gave me confidence that I could hold my own with anyone. Jack and I became good friends, most improbably to be sure, I suppose another older brother I didn't know I was missing. We had a lot of laughs, disappearing on projects if things were slow to have a couple beers, one time getting high on weed on the roof of a hangar at the airport, then dissolving into giggles during a concrete pour as Mac fumed. But Jack also plumbed me up on occasions.

I hadn't seen him for several weeks but found him at the bar of the Hofbrau on O'Farrell, chatting up the waitress, one of his regular lays. When she was gone, he said, "I figured you'd be around. What happened on that job?" "The labor foreman and one of his men climbed a rebar column before the cage was welded; he cut his guy wires and it went over on them. Killed him." "Tough. But he should've known better." "Yeah, but I keep wondering if he did it because he thought I said it was okay or something." Jack looked at me, stretched, finished his Rolling Rock. "Come on, let's get out of here." Outside we walked a ways up the street, then he grabbed by the lapels and slammed me against a storefront. "Did you tell him they were welded?" "No, of course not, because they weren't." "Then stop this fucking around inside your head, blaming yourself for things you know you didn't do. You've got enough to feel bad about, everybody does, without inventing shit." He gave me an added push, then continued on toward Powell, standing on the corner watching a cable car clang by, looking around at the people and the buildings and the lights aglow in the beginning fog. "Isn't it wonderful? I think it's wonderful."

Richard Snodgrass

Moving the Hat

In a few years with a different testing lab I was promoted to Field Supervisor; when the company president discovered he couldn't trust the management staff and he was afraid for his engineering license, I was promoted to report directly to him. The years of working as an inspector had taught me some important life lessons. I had learned to walk onto an unfamiliar project in the middle of a concrete pour, fifty men or more busy working around me, and stand there, blank faced, watching what was going on. Later a surveyor told me the men thought I must be the toughest son-of-a-bitch in the valley, the way I would just stand there; truth was, I was trying to figure out what the hell was going on. I learned to look a guy in the eyes, maybe somebody I had shared a joke or a cup of coffee, and tell him that his work was wrong and had to come out, a determination that might cost him his job. I learned to say No.

Most important of all, I learned that if I was going to survive in this work, I would need to maintain a careful balance, and it wasn't only to keep from falling off a beam or a piece of planking over an otherwise open floor. It meant a balance between who I was and who I wasn't, what I could and couldn't do. There were times and situations in my young life when I had considered myself tough, almost a tough guy. Hah! Now I daily interacted with men who were truly tough who, if they took a mind to, could destroy me, who lived in and understood the potential for violence that surrounds us every day. Moreover, I interacted with men (women were just beginning to be seen in the building trades) with skills working with materials that I could barely comprehend much less perform. On the other hand, I possessed abilities and knowledge that others didn't have, and that I had a role to play, my piece of the puzzle in putting a building together, that others appreciated and even relied on. It required that I be true to myself, who I was, what I could do, no more and no less; and I found that if I was true to that self, I earned and achieved the respect of others. Respect for myself.

Richard Snodgrass

Moving the Hat

The time I spent working as a construction inspector did much to form and solidify my personality. It reinforced certain character traits, brough them to the fore: my natural inquisitiveness, my in-born suspicion of how a thing appears on the surface, my dubiousness of what people tell me until I see it for myself. My tendency as a loner. It helped define how I handled myself in situations, how I handled my relationships with other people, it helped define my image of myself. It even influenced the clothes I wore, the way I dressed. It seems silly to reflect on it now, but I had always admired cowboy or roper boots but never felt entitled to wear them; now I felt legitimate, I never wore regular shoes after that. And then there was the hat. Construction workers tend to take great store in their hard hats, they mark the type of work you do. By their hats ye shall know them. More to the point, I got used to wearing a hat all day, and felt exposed after work without something on my head. My father always wore a hat, setting himself apart from other businessmen in Pittsburgh with his tall-crowned gray Stetson known as a rancher's model; he used his hat as a prop, taking it off for significance, using it to punctuate a point. In the early years of marriage I tried a variety of different headgear: a Greek fisherman's cap (Carol said, "Aye, matey); a French beret ("Oui, oui, hand me a baguette"), an Irish tweed flat cap ("Sure and begorrah!"), a cloth bucket hat ("Don't be ridiculous"). Then one Friday evening walking through the first floor of I. Magnin, Carol said, "There goes your hat." Sure enough, a dark tan Stetson, low crown, stiff rolled brim, an Indian motif headband, suggestive of a gambler but not quite. I was in love. I followed the hat down the aisles until I cornered the wearer, a pudgy non-descript guy who looked afraid I was going to attack him. I said the immortal words of the old vaudeville song, "Where did you get that hat?" Turned out if was from Orvis. Being Friday evening when the stores were open, we went there and I got my own. On Monday when I first wore it into the office, Arthur, the young Creole lab assistant said, "Snaa-grass, with a hat like that you should have you a string of girls."

Moving the Hat

In the years after I graduated from Berkeley, through living with the hippies, all the various jobs, the time as a building inspector and then a supervisor, I continued to write, keeping to my three-to-four hours every day. Though I wasn't much good. I had a few poems published, put together a collection, but it never went anywhere. I wanted to get away from poetry, but my love of Rilke, Neruda, and the Spanish surrealists kept getting the better of me, the urge reoccurring like a persistent rash:

> Your fear likes you. He sits
> At the top of tall ladders,
> Smiling: "Are you coming?";
> Or stands in a gang of teenage boys,
> Encountered on an unfamiliar street.
>
> He is too tall, sticks out, as flabby
> as you seem in morning mirrors.
> His complexion is a sickly green;
> His hair is falling out. You smell
> body odor and bad breath up close. . . .

Eventually I admitted to myself that poetry wasn't my strength; besides, I knew I would always come out lacking in comparison to De. No, except for an occasional lapse, I committed to the prose form, I was most at home in its subtleties of rhythm and construction. The problem was to find the subjects that drove me to want to say something. I wrote a novel *called Hammer Into Anvil* (the title was the best part) about two casual friends who goad each other into trying to blow up the Bay Bridge; I wrote a book of interconnected stories about some folk musicians living in a deserted mansion in Pacific Heights, but couldn't make it work. I began to find myself in some stories about old mining towns in the Sierras, but recognized what I was actually writing were stories from the mill towns where I grew up. I finally found my voice with a story about a trio of friends who had gone to high school together, walking along the main street of their town, after having watched another friend win the Super Bowl, a story that eventually found its way in one of my Books of Furnass, *Holdin On*, entitled "Almost A Shutout."

Richard Snodgrass

Moving the Hat

The day before Christmas eve, I was getting ready to drive to the Oregan coast, going to visit the home of a girl I was dating, and stopped down at the contractor's office before lunch to check with Mac or Jack in case there was something they needed me to look at. The contractor's office was in the basement of a nearby building, sharing space with heating ducts and electrical cables and water pipes. But today the offices were empty. To make sure, I stuck my head in the project manager's office. His desk was empty, but Carol, the jobsite secretary was at hers, eating a sandwich, her head tilted mimicking me.

"Oh," I said, surprised, straightening up. Clearing my throat. "Hi. Nobody around?" "I'm around." "Er, yes. That's true." "Are you saying I'm a nobody?" She was wearing a dark blue silk blouse buttoned up to her neck like a present all wrapped up waiting to be opened, her dark brown hair swept up in a stylish bouffant. Given how shy I was usually around pretty girls, I was surprised at myself, pleased, how quickly I had a comeback. "Nah. I always figured you were the brains of the outfit. Your boss is just the figurehead." I saw her at the weekly status meetings and whenever I came to talk to the project manager, but I had only spoken to her once before. It was at the contractor's Christmas party the past weekend; at one point I found myself standing beside her, watching several couples dancing. She looked at me skeptically, said, "I suppose you're too staid to dance," and walked away. Staid?

I had my new Pentax with me, trying to get familiar with it to take some pictures in Oregon. Carol nodded toward it: "Are you a photographer?" "I used to be," I said, trying to be cool, "back in my hometown." "And where is this hometown?" she asked, dabbing ladylike at the corners of her mouth with a paper napkin. "Beaver Falls, Pennsylvania." It turned out she was from Lock Four, on the other side of Pittsburgh. For a few minutes we talked about living in San Francisco compared to Western Pennsylvania. Finally I said, "So, where is everybody?" "They're all out celebrating and they didn't take me," she pouted. Inspiration! "Why don't we go celebrate?" "I can't just leave." "Sure, you can, you're with the inspector."

Richard Snodgrass

Moving the Hat

We went down the block to the King Kole, the favorite drinking spot of the jobsite where I learned she and Mac often went for drinks after work. I also learned that, for a petite young woman barely five-foot tall, she could drink most guys under the table. We talked through most of the afternoon relating to each other how we got to San Francisco: she had worked for Alcoa in Pittsburgh but wanted something more, loaded up her red MG convertible and, with a side trip to Taliesin in Arizona—she loved Frank Lloyd Wright—came on to San Francisco. Her first day she put on her beatnik clothes and stood in front of the Coexistence Bagel Shop in North Beach, repeating to herself, "I'm here. I'm really here." However, there was the matter of earning a living; she tested off the charts for typing and shorthand, definitely executive secretary material, but chose this job because she liked being the one girl among 367 guys.

I made my trip to Oregon, but couldn't get her out of my thoughts, singing to myself repeatedly the latest release by the Beatles about having just seen a face I can't forget. We dated for a couple of months, going nightly for drinks and dinner, with sleepovers at her place afterward. As dawn lifted over the East Bay hills I would drive through the still deserted streets back to my place on Stanyan Street above the Haight with that delicious feeling of a lover the morning after. In two months we decided to get married—why wait for the obvious? We drove in my blue VW to Carson City, Nevada for the license and blood test, then to a Justice of the Peace in Gardnerville, though we had to wait a couple of hours, he was out retrieving a body from a drowning. That night we honeymooned at an out-of-season ski lodge, with a steak dinner and plenty to drink in the otherwise deserted dining room. It was weeks later we learned that after our dinner the cook went berserk, stabbed several employees, grabbed a hatched and headed for the cabin of the newlyweds. As fate would have it, a Sherrif's deputy was passing by and shot him on our doorstep. We knew nothing of it, passed out, though noticed in the morning the wait staff kept watching us. We thought it was because we were such a cute couple.

Richard Snodgrass

Moving the Hat

Our first apartment was on the slopes of Russian Hill looking out over the Marina at the Golden Gate and the Marin hills beyond. It was the garden apartment in a building with pretensions to be a Tuscan villa. The Mediterranean theme was carried out in the apartment: walls and ceiling painted white, with one large open room featuring picture windows at one end and several decorator pillars at the other, the bedroom with the bathroom shunted off to one side. It was very atmospheric and glamorous; every few days the klaxons called from the bridge to announce the arrival of a spring fog to blanket the city. Unfortunately, the owners of the building who lived upstairs had a teenage son enamored of the Ventures; the twang of surfing guitars reverberated through the ceiling dominating our life every afternoon and evening. When we asked if he could turn it down, the reply was, "Boys will be boys." I responded in mature fashion by sticking my fist through one of the decorator pillars.

On a walk to get away from the noise, we happened on a For Rent sign on a luxury building at the top of Union Street and thought, Just on a lark. . . . The Chinese houseboy from the residence next door who showed us the apartment took a liking to us, and convinced the owners to let us have it. The owners kept the three-story, twelve-unit Victorian building to assure control of their neighbors, so the rent was reasonable considering; the apartment had been renovated by Skidmore, Owings, and Merrill, with double doors from the Spreckels Mansion, grass-cloth wallpaper, a mural of Versailles painted on the dining room wall, and green shag carpet throughout. Our first night after Bekins delivered our furniture, we sat on the floor amid the boxes, light from the streetlamps and passing cars coming through the louvered windows, the jubilant clang of the cable cars rattling by on Hyde Street, drinking champagne to toast ourselves for making the big time. For the next five years or so we were the image of the good life in San Francisco, that darling couple, all the more charming I suppose because of the six-foot-two-and-a-half construction inspector with the five-foot-tall executive secretary. The difference in height never occurred to me though I should have realized that what I saw most of Carol was the top of her head.

Richard Snodgrass

Moving the Hat

After I had graduated from Berkeley and moved to San Francisco, I continued to hear sporadically from De. From what I pieced together, his life was in upheaval, though he put a good face on things, ever the would-be wild man, for his impressionable younger brother. For one thing, the requests to give readings had dried up considerably. Interest in *Heart's Needle* was dwindling, especially after Robert Lowell published *Life Studies*; no matter that De's innovations had influenced *Life Studies*, Robert Lowell was. . .well, Robert Lowell. By this time, most anyone who wanted to hear De read had done so, and interest wouldn't return until he had a new book. Which was a whole other problem. He was beginning to question what he wanted his poetry to be, what he wanted his career to be. He had discovered through his many readings that he really liked performing, liked the instant gratification of an appreciative audience, and that he was good at it. A natural; charming, charismatic. Able to pull in an audience with a tilt of his head, a knowing look, a little smile. He began to write poems, not as Rilke would say out of necessity, but from what De thought would sound good for him to perform. He wondered if he could get good enough playing the lute to give concerts of his translations of troubadour songs; he continued to try to write plays, and hung out with the Detroit theater companies. Now that his marriage to Jan was headed toward divorce, and his love affair with Tibby had dissipated, he wrote me that he had begun to date the young actresses from the Vanguard and the avant-garde Unstabled.

Then I made the transgressions of transgressions. I thought that because De offered criticism of poems I sent him, that I could offer criticism of poems he sent me. Silly me. When I wrote in response to a couple new poems that I thought he was starting to imitate himself, he didn't write again for over a year—and then mainly to say he had a new love in his life: "I have a new girl named Camille Rykowski (honest! – her father was a Polish cop who played the violin). She's the least glamorous and most affectionate woman I've gone with in a long time. I may finally be getting intelligent (don't bet on it.). . . ."

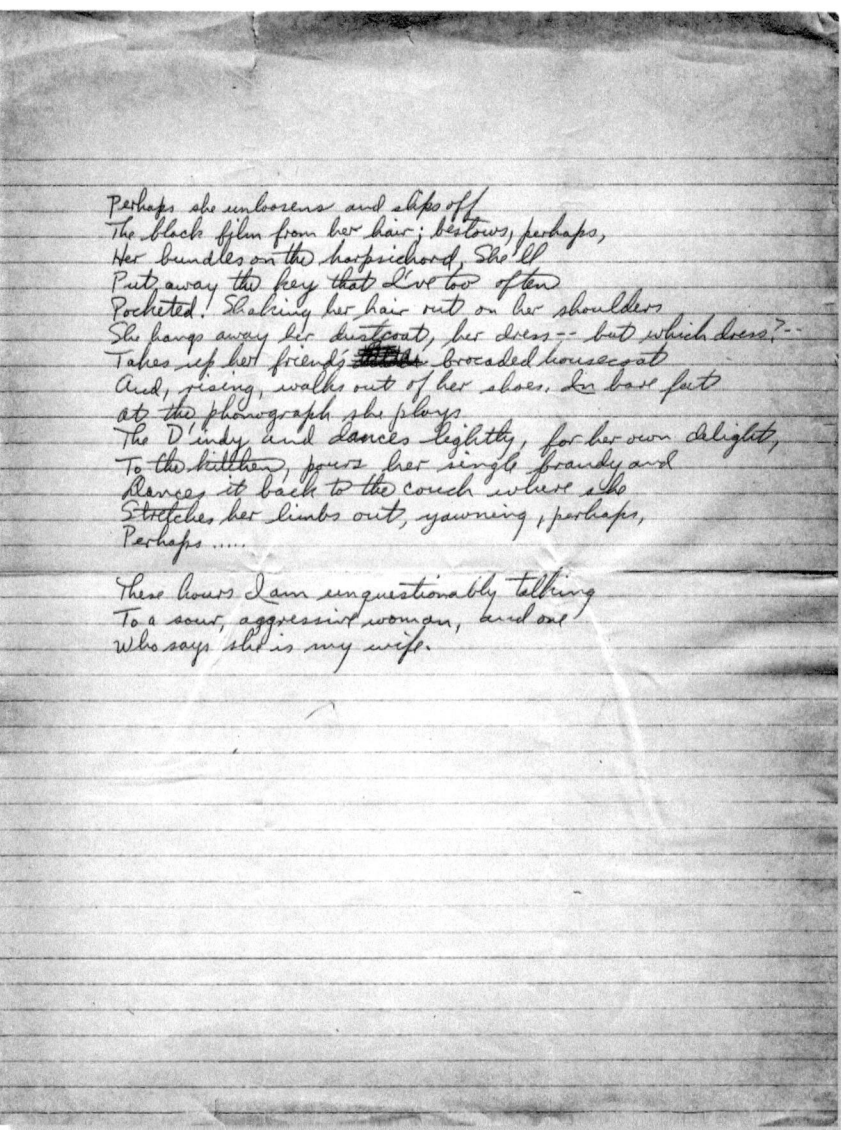

Perhaps she unloosens and slips off
The black film from her hair; bestows, perhaps,
Her bundles on the harpsichord. She'll
Put away the key that I've too often
Pocketed. Shaking her hair out on her shoulders
She hangs away her dustcoat, her dress -- but which dress? --
Takes up her friend's ~~silks~~ brocaded housecoat
And, rising, walks out of her shoes. Her bare feet
at the phonograph she plays
The D'indy and dances lightly, for her own delight,
To the kitchen, pours her single brandy and
Dances it back to the couch where she
Stretches her limbs out, yawning, perhaps,
Perhaps....

These hours I am unquestionably talking
To a sour, aggressive woman, and one
Who says she is my wife.

Moving the Hat

Maybe it was working as a construction inspector that not only required I see things as they were, but that I speak up and say so, often in the face of someone who didn't want to hear it. Or maybe it was the influence of a couple of surrogate big brothers I worked with on jobsites, who supported and encouraged me to be myself, to stand up for myself, to not hold back when I knew I was right. Whatever, my differences with De continued to grow. It was increasingly apparent that he had never seen me beyond someone who needed his guidance, that he considered me incapable of having thoughts and feelings different than his own, that if I did express ideas different than his own I was to be avoided or ignored, cast out from the Select. The first clear break between us came at our father's funeral, when he declared that our mother had welcomed father's terminal illness because she finally had him right where she wanted him, totally under her control. When I tried to lighten the mood and said, "Oh, come on, De, you don't really believe that, do you?" he turned on me in a rage, how dare I speak to him that way, said I was blind and stupid and a fool. Well, so much for that.

I hoped that we could still reach an accommodation, a mutual understanding and respect, and thought that Carol might help ease things between us as a go-between, a stabilizing influence. But when De stopped off in San Francisco on one of his reading tours, the introductory meeting with Carol didn't go well. We took him to our favorite restaurant on Nob Hill, a small intimate place decorated like an English club with hunter green walls and paintings of hounds and foxes, with a low ceiling and tables close together. Sadly, De took over the room—was he drunk, or nervous about seeing us?—talking in his performer's voice as he told us, and everyone else within hearing, stories of some TV appearance where he was attacked by the black poet LeRoy Jones—he was sure it was because De showed up with a "colored" girl on his arm—and Alan Ginsberg became his new best friend. In the car after we returned De to his hotel, Carol said, "Your brother surely does love W. D. Snodgrass, doesn't he?"

Moving the Hat

...because I still didn't get it yet, but that's not true either, because I knew it well enough by this time, I had had plenty of examples, that all his jive talk of "Rich-Baby" and "You wild-man you" and "You're going for it, man, you're flying" was simply that, jive talk, aimed at himself, I knew it well enough by this time but I didn't want to believe it, I was more than willing to make excuses for him on the hope that among all that hyperbole and over-exuberance and fancy-dance was a modicum of feeling and affection directed not at himself, not just to hear himself talk, loving as he did the sound of his own voice, meant to jack himself up and in a way jack himself off, rather than to convey his good wishes and pleasure to see someone, namely me, because that was who he was, that was what drove him, because what drove him made it impossible for him to see beyond himself, he never could, even as a boy, a child, he looked at the world but all he could see was himself looking back at himself, not just a reflection of himself but truly himself, no distinction between what he looked at and what he was looking with, all was one, De, world without end, amen, even if he might want to see someone else, acknowledge another's presence, he was fundamentally unable to do so, it was totally against his nature, all that he relied on, depended on, he was trapped within himself, a man in a bunker as it were as he would write about later in life when I think on some level of his mind he finally realized it about himself, unable to change and perhaps not truly wanting to, having seen the world that way for so long, not wanting to change but perhaps needing to justify in the description of the horrific transgressions of others the failings he was aware of but couldn't directly admit to in his own life, a man who loved to perform because for that brief instant of others' adulation he could feel that he lived not in the world around him but within himself alone....

"Are you through?" Marty says.

"Yeah, I think I got it out of my system."

"Good. Let's get back to your snippets...."

Richard Snodgrass

Moving the Hat

It was Camille who turned out to be the go-between with De and me, the stabilizing influence—until she wasn't. Shortly after she and De were married, Camille took over most of the letter-writing to the San Francisco Snodzies, as she referred to us, long, snappy, chatty, funny, zingy letters every few weeks that she called Snot-O-Grams, with De only occasionally adding comments at the end or in the margins. De had been appointed a cultural ambassador by the State Department, making a number of trips to Russia and middle European countries to give readings and visit writer's unions. Camille usually went along on these trips and her letters were mini-travelogs, filled with her bouncy impressions and stories of their adventures in foreign lands. Her boundless enthusiasm was enough right there to make reticent Carol suspicious of her.

All of Carol's misgivings about De and Camille, justified or not, played out that fall during a trip back East to visit our families. De was teaching at the University of Syracuse and they were living in a farmhouse near a village called Erieville. Appropriately enough. They met us after dark at a crossroads to lead us along the country roads. Camille bounded out of their car to greet us; what she lacked in De's definition of glamorous was made up for by her eagerness and infectious energy. She was my age, fifteen years younger than De, a strawberry blonde with broad Eastern European features dusted with freckles, greenish eyes. Carol bristled as Camille hugged her, called her "Sisterwoman." De, in a full beard, was looking like an Orthodox priest; he reached out to hug Carol but she waved him away. At their house, in the confusion of unloading our car, their black Great Dane bolted out of the garage where it was kept, prancing about us. When the dog wouldn't come to him, De grabbed it, threw it down and started to beat it. "Stop that," Carol said, "he didn't mean anything." De glared at her. "You have to discipline a dog this size, show who's in control." Carol put her arms around its neck, the dog sitting nearly as tall as she was. "He's just an excitable boy, isn't he?" The black dog stayed close to her as we collected our suitcases and followed Camille into the house. But De announced they needed kindling, said good-night, took his axe and began chopping furiously.

Richard Snodgrass

Moving the Hat

The days during our visit set the pattern for all my subsequent visits to De and Camille's over the years: after breakfast De would disappear upstairs to his study for the day, reappearing only to chop firewood or do some other chore, it understood that he was still working and not to be spoken to unless he spoke first. Meanwhile Carol would curl up on the couch in the living room wrapped in a blanket whether she need it or not, reading whatever book she found handy. That left me sitting in the kitchen with Camille as she did the breakfast dishes or started dinner; later I would go with her as she ran errands to Manlius or Cazenovia, or we would take walks up the hill into the woods behind the house, talking about anything and everything and laughing a lot, at ease with each other from the first morning. After De was done working and we were allowed to talk to him again, we had dinner while listening to his choice of music, often Alfred Deller, Ewan MacColl, or Ralph Vaughn Willians, all conversation on hold when it came to meaningful passages. Later we gathered in the living room drinking wine as De told stories or gave his analysis of people and their motives while noodling on his lute. At times we tried to work up my accompanying him on a dumbeck to his readings of Whitman, but it never really worked.

The most important thing to come out of that first visit, besides confirming Carol's dislike of De and Camille, was my introduction to a book lying on their coffee table: Wright Morris' *God's Country and My People*. The book alternated a page of Morris' writing facing a page with a photograph he took as a younger man, telling stories of his home place on the Great Plains of Nebraska and the people he had known there. I was as excited as when I first discovered James Joyce's *Dubliners*, Walker Evans' or Eugene Atget's photographs, Ken Kesey's *Sometimes a Great Notion*. I hadn't considered photography seriously since before college, concentrating on my writing instead, but here were both mediums, working together. I could hardly wait to get back to San Francisco to try photographing again. As we drove away, Carol gave her last word on the visit: "Poor Camille. She hasn't figured out yet that she got the wrong brother."

Richard Snodgrass

Moving the Hat

On a Saturday morning a few weeks after we got back from our trip East, Carol came with me as I went downtown to Brooks Camera. I had no idea what camera I was looking for, trusting that I would know it when I saw it, and fell in love with a used twin-lens Rolleiflex, which we named the Old Man. Our apartment was only a few blocks from the San Francisco Art Institute, instrumental in nurturing the Bay Area Figurative Movement, the painters who helped bring me to the area in the first place, and I signed up for several night school classes to refresh my darkroom techniques. I also took a class with Linda Connor, a prominent young photographer in the area's active photography scene. She in turn directed me to the workshops of Oliver Gagliani, not only a master technician of the Zone System but simply a master photographer. For the next five years or so I studied with Oliver, becoming a close friend as well as a teaching assistant for his Virginia City Workshops. I discovered that one of my main subjects were the interiors of people's houses, showing how people lived, the stage settings of their lives; the Zone System techniques Oliver taught me, using extreme expansions or contractions in developing the film to photograph a room lit only with natural light, whatever filtered in through the windows, allowed me to capture the spirit of the people who lived in those rooms. Weekends, with Carol keeping me company, I would drive into the Sierras to the old mining towns. I would set up my camera and start to photograph; invariably someone would come out of their house to ask what I was doing, and after telling them and chatting a while I would ask them if I could photograph inside their house. More often than not, they would say okay, and we would sit around drinking coffee during my long, sometimes 15 minute, exposures. On our next trip back east I took along the camera and tripod, photographing my family's house as well as De and Camille's. When I later mailed the Erieville images to De, he wrote, "Holy Jupiter, are ever a photographer! These pictures you took in our house simply flattened us—you were lumphing about so nonchalantly we had no idea you were doing anything like that!. . . I got to wondering, is my house really that frightening???. . . ."

Richard Snodgrass

Moving the Hat

I thought of myself as an artist who had to work in construction to earn a living. It was disheartening when I figured out the reason other artists didn't take me seriously was they considered me a construction worker with hobbies. Sigh.

About this time, I seemed to enter a period when the world didn't help me much to determine which direction I should go in life. When the balance of events certainly seemed weighted toward the negative side of things. To gain some legitimacy, as well as open the possibility of a career change, I went to graduate school for an MFA in Photography at the prestigious California College of Arts and Crafts in Oakland, sneaking off to classes on my rounds to various jobsites. The degree lost its luster, however, when for my graduation presentation I showed the same images I had at my introductory show two years earlier—when the faculty agreed I wasn't an artist and suggested I transfer to a school for journalism—now at my final show praising me for how far I had developed under their tutelage. Oh sure. I also learned that there were currently six openings nationwide for photography instructors and 250 MFA photography graduates. So much for a career change. I figured as long as I had to work at something else, I should make as much money as I could, and applied for several openings for a resident inspector on major projects, each time losing out at the last minute. I submitted novels for publication, poems to little magazines, sent letters seeking an agent. I put together a manuscript of my short stories and photographs of the Gold Country and sent it to a major publisher I had met and corresponded with; after several go-rounds he ultimately turned it down for reasons, he said, even he didn't understand. I told friends that I always thought I would wallpaper my bathroom with my rejection slips, I just hadn't realized I would have such a large bathroom. It turned out that the many rejections took more of a toll on Carol than on me. She told me later that the thing she couldn't stand about me was that things never quite worked out for me; but if that wasn't bad enough, every time I got turned down I bounced right back up again and went on. She hated that, couldn't understand that, drove her crazy.

Richard Snodgrass

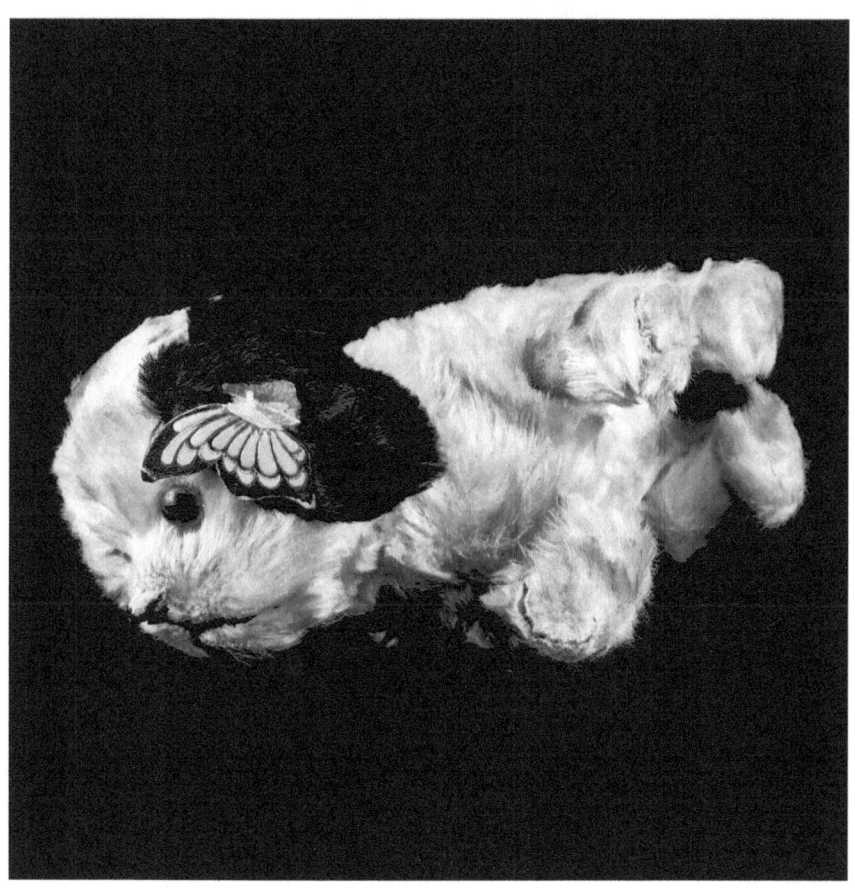

Moving the Hat

It took me a few years to grasp the other side of Carol's "wrong brother" observation, but I asked her about it after the divorce. Yes, she had wanted to be married to a famous writer, which she had finally determined I would never be; she thought she would be good at it, being the gatekeeper, taking care of the correspondence, minding the house and all—certainly better than she thought Camille was. If she hadn't disliked De so much, she would have suggested a switch. Whatever, the cracks in our marriage were probably much more basic. Carol found sex to be a sticky business; though she went through with it with much the same attitude that made her a good executive secretary. As for me, I had yearnings.

Intellectually, I knew Carol was a good wife, physicality aside, and my best friend. I was determined to make it work between us, to overcome my desires and appreciate Carol's other qualities. I learned that the Cal Extension was offering a night school class in writing crime fiction, and we signed up for it. I thought this was something we could do together, write crime fiction; we both loved detective novels, it would draw us closer. As fate would have it, at the first class we attended there was a gorgeous, life-of-the-party dark-haired girl sitting up front attracting a gaggle of admirers. I did my best not to look at her; Carol had great fun mimicking her, and I tried to laugh. Later, during a break, the girl with several admirers was ahead of us walking down the corridor. From the way she kept looking back, it seemed she was aware of me too. But I consciously turned away to look at Carol, I could do this, I would be true to my wife.

Then all my good intentions went to hell the very next morning at work when the president of the company came to my desk and said, "Richard, you need to go home and pack a bag. You're going to Seattle."

Richard Snodgrass

Moving the Hat

It was a seven-office construction testing lab, a sister-company to my own, with offices extending from Olympia to Marysville and Whitby Island, as well as the Hanford nuclear power plant. Monday morning the management team—manager, laboratory supervisor, field supervisor—all quit and walked out, a move to cripple the company so they could purchase it cheap. Corporate told me to try to hold things together until they could hire replacements—here's a company pickup, lists of employees and projects, and a map, off you go, do good! Amazingly, I seemed to know intuitively what to do, how to handle myself and situations that came up. Apparently my father had taught me more about business dealings than I realized, and I found myself thinking in tight spots, what would my father do? The first order of business was to make contact with each of the twenty inspectors in the field. I spent the first few days going to each project, finding the inspector, and introducing myself. Now, it was March and cold in the Northwest, and I cut quite a figure in the clothes I normally wore in chilly weather in San Francisco: a sheepskin coat, gambler's Stetson, walking-heel ropers. The California Sharpy they called me, not necessarily a compliment. The thing was, I realized I could use the persona to my advantage, stand out from the ordinary. I told each inspector that I was there to save their job and provide them with backup; that I ran a thirty-plus crew of inspectors in San Francisco, and that I had probably encountered any situation they would ever come across; I told them I was committed to helping them, to holding the company together, and I asked them to be committed to me, to give us a chance. And damn if they didn't. It certainly helped that on the first job I went to, a parking garage in downtown Tacoma, the young towheaded inspector who looked all of fourteen was in the middle of a heated situation with the rebar foreman. I asked to see the drawings, looked at the rebar the inspector had rejected, and pointed out an easy fix for him to present to the foreman that I was confident the project engineer would approve. Situation resolved. Word spread quickly through the company that the California Sharpy was here to save the day. Wow, did I think I was something! And maybe I was, too.

Moving the Hat

My other principal stroke of intuition was to realize I needed to get close to whoever knew the most about the workings of the company. The bookkeeper. Brilliant. She was a young widow about my age supporting two boys, a Scorpio, a sturdy voluptuous Scandinavian with a knowing and mischievous look and long flowing hair. Of course she did. After talking to her on the phone fifteen times a day for a couple of weeks about troublesome clients and what the company needed, I asked her if she was lunchable. She chuckled. I took her to a fancy restaurant in Bellevue where she looked at the menu and asked, "Richard, what's a quickie?" I explained what a quiche was; she laughed at herself. After a few more weeks, I asked her if she was drinkable. Which, of course, turned into supperable. Eventually, it became bedable.

Before I arrived the company had been losing money for over a year, the management team running the company into the ground to make it more affordable when Corporate wanted to unload it. Within two months, under my management, aided with the bookkeeper's insights, we were breaking even. In three months, we were turning a profit—only a couple thousand dollars a month, but a lot better than it had been. I was pretty damn proud of myself. And there were women. The company flew me back to San Francisco each weekend whenever I wanted to make the trip, but it was apparent my marriage was ending. Absence makes the heart grow fonder, or just the reverse. I felt a stranger in my own apartment, The City no longer seemed to have anything to do with me. After being as they say True to Carol for seven years, the flood gates opened. In addition to the bookkeeper, Suzie the office manager from my own company, a foxy statuesque blonde ten years older than me, flew up one Friday to spend the weekend in my bed. There was the waitress from the motel coffee shop, a woman I met in the motel bar, others. I would get off the plane at Sea-Tac on a Sunday evening, see the Haida drawings in the terminal, and feel I was home. I would tell myself I had to try harder with Carol, forget about the others. But back in my motel room in Tacoma, I would make a phone call to whoever I knew was available—anyway.

Richard Snodgrass

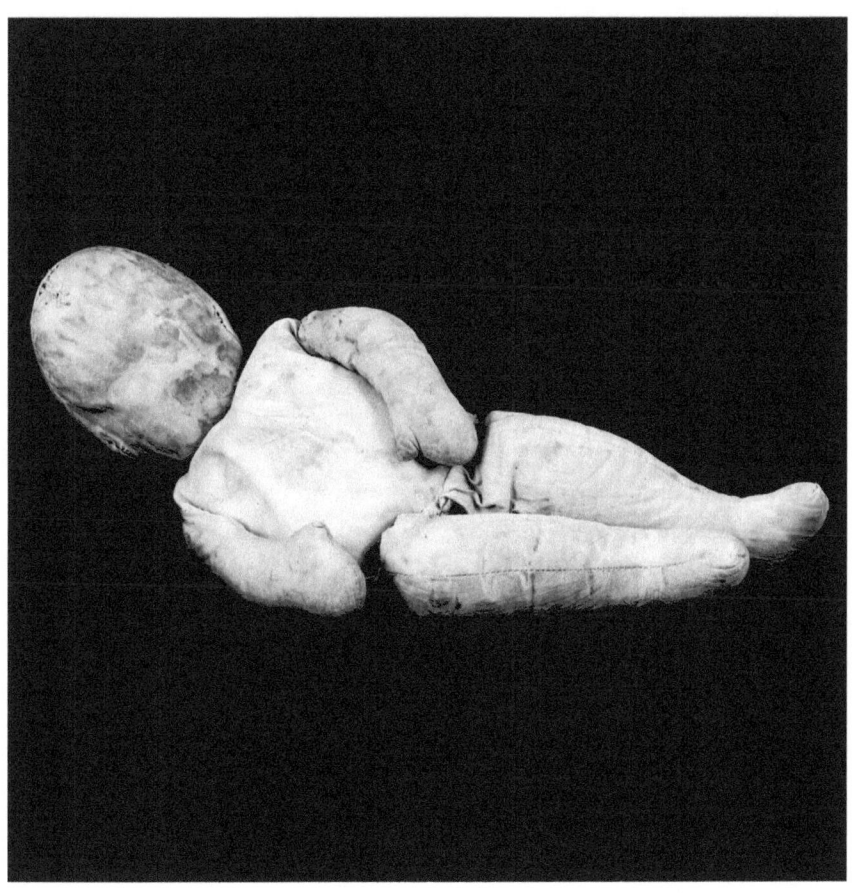

"Goody for you," Marty says. "But what does all that have to do with being an artist?"

Exactly.

I thought from time to time about my writing, my photography, but the balance in my life had definitely shifted to my job; the truth was that I was having way too much fun. For the first time in my life I felt competent and confident, I was The Man; I had power and control managing the company, and I seemed to be good at it. I gave up my 3 to 4 hours a day writing on the rationale that I didn't have a block of time to develop ideas. As for photography, in a Seattle camera store I happened on 3 used lenses for the single-lens Rolleiflex I bought before my Northwest saga began. On my next weekend trip to San Francisco I brought the camera and tripod back with me to try out the lenses, photographing the shadows in a park one early morning, but I knew something was missing.

I was considering moving to Seattle, I felt more at home there than I had any place I had ever lived, but the president of my company said, "Don't do it, Richard," aware of something he couldn't tell me, and after eight months I returned to San Francisco. A few weeks later, Carol and I sat down one Sunday evening and divided up our possessions, still good friends. The following week I helped her move into her own apartment on Polk Street. Before I left Seattle one of my last duties was to find a new manager for the company, but after a few months he wasn't working out; Corporate sent me back to hold the company together again until they decided what to do. I fell back into all my old habits, picking up my sexual relationships again. Corporate, however, had had enough with the company; they instructed me to conduct tours for potential buyers. When the sale was final, I had the task of telling the bookkeeper she was the one employee who wasn't going with the new owners. Congratulations, Richard, your transformation was complete: I had developed the Corporate Heart, which meant no heart at all. Back in San Francisco, I felt bereft of my home, my position in the world. The employees of my company treated me like they didn't know me. And maybe they didn't. It was becoming quite apparent that I didn't know myself.

Richard Snodgrass

Moving the Hat

And what I did know of myself, I didn't like. It finally sunk in the degree that I was being untrue to myself, how badly I betrayed the thing I loved most: art. My art. I had succumbed to one of the oldest temptations in the book; I had been tested as surely as any saint in a cave with the pleasures of the material world, with the addiction to strokes to the ego—and I had failed miserably. For years I had criticized my brother for letting fame go to his head and damage his work, for letting the attention of an adoring audience get the better of him, for doing anything to keep the flattery coming, and here I had done it myself—not on the grand scale of the literary world, but in a dinky testing lab tucked away in the far northwest corner of the country. How sad. How pathetic. I redevoted myself to my own work, not the company's; I trained myself to live on five-hours' sleep a night, writing for several hours before going to the office in the morning, spending my evenings in the darkroom. Among the images I worked on were the ones I had taken in the park before I left Tacoma. They were competent enough, full of early morning extremes of light and shadow, moody, but as I suspected something was missing. And I had an insight that changed the direction and intention of the rest of my life. Those photographs didn't work for me, held no interest for me, because they didn't contain a story, either individually or as a series, they gave no sense of a human or mystical element, a feeling that something had happened or would happen here, a narrative that could be inherent even in a single image. I realized that was what I had always looked for in a photograph, beyond the beauty that could be achieved through the photographic process, why I liked one image and not another; and that was what always interested me in a scene or subject to photograph, what held my attention to go through the laborious process of making a fine art photograph. In that moment I realized that all my writing, all my photographing, had had the same goal: to find the best way to tell a story, and to find the stories to tell. Plain and simple: I was a storyteller.

Richard Snodgrass

Moving the Hat

On my last visit to Beaver Falls a couple years earlier, I took my camera and tripod, photographing around the town but mainly in my family's house. Now I had an idea: a book of photographs that showed the house as it functioned in De's poems, the darkness, the clutter and chaos, the setting where he wrote his mother moved "by habit, hungering and blind." I was looking for stories to tell; well, there were stories aplenty in that house. Maybe I would write something to go with the images; maybe I could use sections of the poems themselves. I knew De was concerned that his work didn't draw the interest it once did; maybe the book I was thinking of could help revive that interest, help his career. Plus, I needed to get away from my company for a while, reset my sensitivities. I had three weeks' vacation coming and I decided to take it.

Back in the house where I was raised, I would set up my camera after breakfast and start to photograph. Mother accused me of taking pictures of all the messes, but I explained I was looking for images of the way people lived. She nodded and smiled as if she knew better. The challenge was the interior of the house was so dark that the exposures could be as long as fifteen, twenty minutes. To keep her occupied, I would give her all the figures regarding my light meter readings, film speed, reciprocity, lens extension, etc., and she would do the calculations. Then we would sit together. "Is it going now?" she'd ask. "Yes, it's going now." To pass the time, I asked her questions about the family, how she and my father met, their early life together, the childhoods of my brother and sisters and me, the things we did together as a family, the things that happened to us, my sister Barbara's death, my father's. And I got a very different perspective of the family than the one De's analytical intervention pulled from me as a teenager. I talked to my mother for the first time in my life—more importantly, I listened to her, and a new world of understanding opened up for me. Rather than the monster that De described, I saw someone with her own heartbreaks and pleasures, strivings and yearnings, weaknesses and strengths. A woman in her own right beyond the term Mother. A person.

Richard Snodgrass

Moving the Hat

After two weeks in Beaver Falls, I borrowed my mother's car and drove to Erieville to see De and Camille. It was the first time I had made the visit without Carol, and I expected it to be looser and probably more fun without her disapproving presence. It was late afternoon when I got there; Camille hurried out the back door. pretty in a pinafore apron over a play outfit, gave me a hug of the long-lost and led me into the house, sitting me down at the kitchen table to keep her company as she made dinner. Just like old times. Talking together as if picking up a conversation from only the week before. When De appeared from upstairs, we did our version of a hug, a hand-grip with a shoulder-bump added. "How goes it, laddie-buck?" "It's good, how're you?" He gave me one of his sidelong, over- the-top-of-his-glasses-looks, as if I should know better than to ask, and we went into dinner. De was looking bushier and more patriarchal than ever, the poet as would-be farmer; he seemed in a good mood and I thought my visit would be a good one. But the conversation soon turned, as it always did, to his wanting to hear the latest follies of Mama Snots.

Instead, I told them of the conversations I had with Mother while I was photographing in the house, particularly about Father's last days. I could see De's aggravation growing as I related the story of Mother and Father laughing when the TV repairman unknowingly sat on the port-a-potty. When I told them that apparently Mother and Father grew close at the end, they even had a favorite TV program, "Twenty Thousand Leagues Under the Sea," that they watched every afternoon, holding hands, De lost it.

"You blind stupid fool!" De said, standing up, tossing his chair aside. "You know the emotional tricks she uses to tie us up in knots."

His dramatics seemed ludicrous. "Oh, come on, De, for fuck's sake, listen to yourself."

Camille gasped. De glared; I stood in case he came at me but he slammed another empty chair out of his way and headed out the back door. I listened to his progress through the workroom and the garage to the outside. In a moment he started howling, heading up to the woods.

"He does that," Camille said. "When he's upset."

"I'd say that's my cue to leave."

"Please don't go."

I was ready to head out to the car, but stopped. Camille looked worried—no, more than that. Afraid.

"Please stay. Tomorrow if you're here he'll act like none of this ever happened, though I'm sure he won't forget it. If you leave now, there'll be just the two of us, he'll rail at me about it for days, getting angrier every time. And if he thinks I didn't support him enough. . . ."

"Does he hit you?"

She looked at her hands in her lap and didn't answer. Instead she told me that somehow De got the idea she was having an affair, maybe with one of his students who sometimes hung out at the house; they said they came to see him but he suspected it was really to see her—he said she was too friendly with them. He had taken to leaving translations of poems he was working on lying around, poems about unfaithful wives, husbands taking their revenge. Often his axe or a hatchet nearby.

"Please. For me."

The next day as Camille predicted, De acted like nothing had happened. The days fell into the easy routine of my earlier visits, De spending the day upstairs working in his study, Camille and I talking in the kitchen, running errands, taking walks together in the woods. I tried, without much success, not to watch her legs in her little white tennis shorts, her ass. When I thought of staying a few days longer, I called my company in San Francisco. Suzie, the office manager, answered the phone but was obviously upset, she'd been trying to reach me. There had been a shake up in the company, the President I reported to had quit over policy, and the vultures were out for me. I would be demoted when I returned to the lowest of the low. Good-bye, Richard, it was a pleasure working with you. Good luck. I hung up, shaken. Camille had hopped up to sit on the edge of the kitchen counter; when I told her, she clapped her hands, her face bursting with delight.

"That's wonderful, Dick! Don't you see? You'll get unemployment, right? Well, now you can spend your time working on your writing and photography, like you always wanted. It's like you got a grant or something." She was swinging her legs like a teenager. "Plus, now you can stay for the party on Saturday."

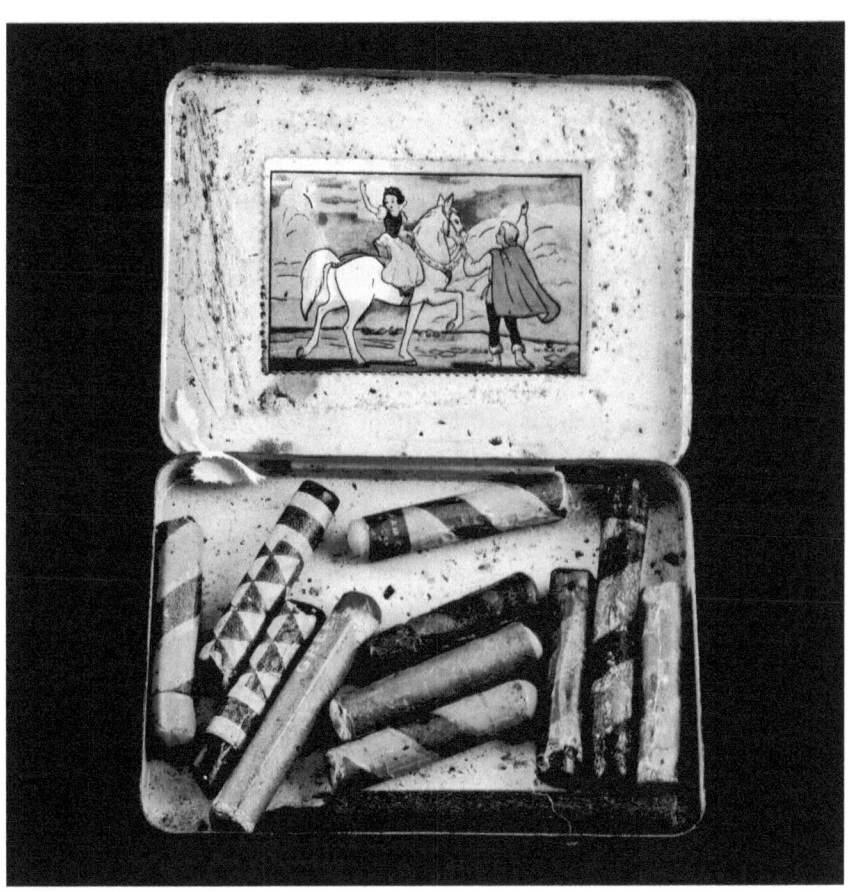

Moving the Hat

It was a small get-together at Don Dykes' farm, a few miles away—Don and his wife Sally, George and Mary Emma Elliott, De and Camille. I had wondered if Camille expected me to sit with her, I got the idea I was a buffer for her from something, but she sat on the couch with Mary Emma and Sally Dike, while I took a spindly captain's chair. De sat on the floor noodling on his lute. Eventually the English Department gossip drifted into whether you could drive under a rainbow. Camille was wearing a white harem-like outfit, shear pants clasped at her ankles, shear top. She watched the discussion for an hour or so, then got up and took her empty beer bottle to the kitchen. I waited a few minutes and followed. I found her squatting beside a washtub full of icy water, her arm submerged past her elbow, rummaging through the bottles on the bottom., "Found it!" she announced and bounced up with another Rolling Rock. She stood close to me, like confiding secret information, tipsier than I first realized. "Talk to George, I told him about your job and he's got a proposition for you." It seemed the Elliotts were leaving at Christmastime for nine months in Europe and wanted to know if I'd house-sit for them. When I spoke to George, he said he'd send me a contract if I was interested. I don't remember much else of the evening; it broke up with Don heading off into the darkness on his tractor to cut hay and everyone else going to their cars. I was ready to follow De and Camille back to their place when Camille left their car and came to mine, the headlights shining through her gauzy outfit like a vision. "We don't have to wait for him." She directed me a long way round, the night air flowing through the open windows as we wound along country roads. Then the road was covered with peepers, tiny baby frogs, thousands of them, hopping up in front of the headlights, bouncing off the hood and windshield. The rain earlier had brought them out, I could feel them squishing under the tires, the road slick. A chorus of chirring, chirring. In a mile or so we were beyond them. After we rolled the windows back down, Camille stretched her arm along the back of the seat, touching my neck. Then she put her hand on my thigh. "Oh Dick, don't you wish we could drive like this forever?" I pushed her hand away, inadvertently slamming it into the dash. "Don't play games with this, Camille. You don't know what you're getting into." We didn't talk the rest of the way home, and when I left in the morning no one saw me off.

Richard Snodgrass

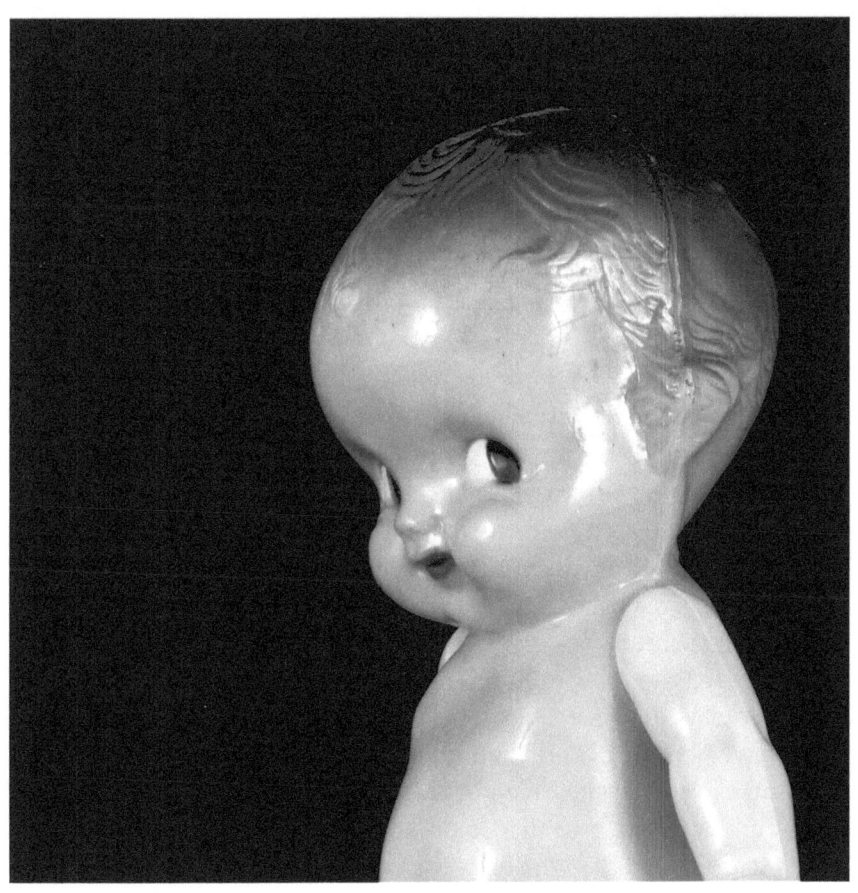

Moving the Hat

Sure enough, when I reported for work after my Eastern trip, I found my pickup truck assigned to someone else, my desk cleaned out, even the cactus on my desktop thrown away. Suzie, I was told, was fired after she talked to me because she talked to me. The dispatcher, an angly guy named Dave who always looked at people somewhere above their left shoulder, with whom I had had many a run-in over the years after I was promoted over him, took great glee in sending me out to cut concrete cores, a dirty and dangerous job working on a scaffold thirty foot high with no safety net. I agreed to go, but told him I wanted to see the new manager when I got back. He was a droopy guy from Corporate named Wilson, wearing an ill-fitting window-pane sport coat who told me to make it quick, he had important things to do. I told him I thought he should consider that although someone had cleaned out my files, did he really think I wouldn't have duplicates of the important ones off site? The ones, for instance, for a certain local hospital that his dispatcher falsely signed approving the foreign steel? No such documents existed, of course, but Wilson didn't know that. He looked at me for a long minute. "What do you want, Snodgrass?" I told him it was very simple: a letter that said my position was eliminated so I could get my unemployment right away; one month's severance; and a written promise that the company wouldn't contest my unemployment when the State called. In twenty minutes I had my two documents and a check. I blew a kiss to Dave the dispatcher and rode off into the sunset.

There followed several happy months of working on my writing and photography. In the evenings I saw Suzie along with several other young women; Carol and I had drinks a few times but one night at a bar she exploded, said I ruined her life, and started flailing at me. My main problem was that the Union Street apartment was expensive, and I had to tap into my savings each month.to make ends meet. Camille had taken to writing to me again as if nothing had happened, and kept reminding me of the Elliotts' offer of a free place to stay for nine months, all I had to do was get there.

Richard Snodgrass

Moving the Hat

George Elliott was pressing me for a decision; he sent me a contract detailing the arrangements, including a $3000 penalty if I backed out. Really, George? Then one Saturday morning after doing some maintenance on Murray, my red VW Hatchback—named for Murray Burns in *A Thousand Clowns*—I was sitting on the front steps of the apartment building with a photography friend, trying to catch a glimpse of the pretty girl in the apartment building across the street. My friend knew my quandary. "Well, Dick, what's it going to be? You going or staying?" And it was as if there was a little toggle switch in my mind's eye, and I watched it snap over to *On*. "I'm going." That was that.

It took a couple of months to clear out the apartment, decide what things I could fit into Murray and what things had to go into storage, what things had to be given away. In case I began to doubt myself as to why I was making what could be a fool's journey, I drew up a list of objectives, the reasons why I was uprooting myself and returning to the East Coast. I called the trip, Dance with the Dragon, after a recent Jefferson Starship album. If you asked me then, I would have said that the Dragon was all the doubts I had about myself, the things I needed to change about myself in order to change my life, to restore the balance in my life and live as an artist. All true. But I also knew on some level of my mind that another dragon I was dealing with was my brother, my relationship with him, my feelings toward him. Things I needed to come to terms with before I could feel I was truly free of him, free of his influence. I would only take those things with me that fit into the back of Murray, leaving enough space for a foam mattress and sleeping bag so I could sleep there at night. On the dashboard I stuck a Dymo label: *Everything that doesn't destroy you makes you stronger*. Really, Richard? Before I left I went out with Jack Martin, the construction foreman, for one last beer. When he asked why I was going I said that among other things I wanted to write a book about my family. He laughed: "Dickie, nobody gives a shit about your family."

Moving the Hat

One morning in early December, 1976, I looked up at the windows of 1120 Union St., Apt, 5, one last time—for the briefest moment I thought I saw, behind the louvers, me looking back at me—got in Murray, and left San Francisco. Though it turned out it wasn't the last time I left San Francisco, over the next half dozen years I left a number of times after coming back for one reason or another, but this was the most significant because it was the first. I decided on a Southern route across the country for fear of snow in the mountain passes and on the Great Plains, taking Interstate 5 down the Central Valley then over to Barstow to pick up Interstate 40 across the Mojave Desert, following parts of old Route 66, though going the wrong direction. As I crossed the Great Divide the radio picked up briefly KDFC, the classical music station I always listened to from Palo Alto, Glenn Gould playing William Byrd's Pavan & Galliard "Lord Salisbury," a favorite, then it was gone. Only static. As if it never was. In Alburquerque, I happened on a concert by the Eagles, taking "Hotel California," "New Kid in Town," and "Desperado" as my anthems; in a Denny's for a mid-day Grand Slam breakfast somewhere in Oklahoma a guy next to me at the counter drew my picture on a napkin for no reason; at an auto parts store in Indiana, the young female clerk said, "You're from California, aren't you?" "How did you know?" "You're the only one in here having fun," then begged to come with me; the last night before Beaver Falls, I sat on a bed in a motel outside Wheeling, West Virginia, watching a Crystal Gayle Christmas Special, listening to the woman next door moan, "Help me, Bob, Oh help me, Bob" as the headboard banged the wall.

A few days later I pulled into the Elliotts at five in the afternoon; Mary Emma greeted me with open arms. She sat me down in the kitchen and wanted to hear all about my trip as she served me homemade corned beef hash, the product of her on-going love affair with her new Cuisinart. When I asked about George she said he was "out" but I heard someone moving around upstairs. After dinner we continued talking as we sipped tumblers of Jack Daniels. It was probably close to midnight when she finally got around to telling me that their plans had changed, that they weren't going.

Moving the Hat

"Wait! They weren't going?" Marty says, a disembodied voice with me under the darkcloth. "The Elliotts cancelled their trip?"

On the groundglass the rubber airplane with a childish face doesn't really look at me, it looks off to the side, mouth slightly open, not as if about to say something but as if it's a mouth breather. Not a good look.

"Seems there was some mix-up with the arrangements. Now they weren't going until April."

"That was four months away."

"I was quite aware."

"And George didn't tell you about it before you left San Francisco?"

"He said later he was afraid to. Matter of fact he was upstairs while Mary Emma and I were talking. He left it to her to break the news."

"So what did you do when you saw him? Hit him?"

No, the position of the toy is wrong, the expression. You can't really tell it's an airplane head-on, either. I reach around the camera into the light tent, try to get it balanced at an angle on the blocks beneath the black velvet cloth lining the tent.

"That's the amazing thing to me, thinking back on it. You would have thought I'd go crazy. Or break down crying. I had given up everything of my life in San Francisco to come there, my apartment, furniture, belongings, everything. There was nothing to go back to. But my only thought was, Okay, this is the situation. Take it by the numbers. How am I going to make this work? I surprised myself, I remained perfectly balanced within myself, centered. Maybe all those years of meditation came to something after all. Castenada. I don't know."

"So, how did you make it work?"

"I set myself up in a spare bedroom. There was a big overstuffed chair where I could put my writing board in my lap, and I'd sit there bundled up in blankets and write more or less around the clock. I can't say I was happy, but I loved the intensity of it, I was living the life of an artist. That's when I wrote *The House with Round Windows*."

There. On the groundglass the toy, canted at an angle, is looking at the viewer, smiling, a happy flyer, full of joy. But where I would ever use such an image in a book of Snippets is beyond me.

"And then there was Camille."

"Of course there was," Marty says.

Richard Snodgrass

Moving the Hat

Camille called the morning after I arrived—Mary Emma said she had called every day for the past week, asking if there was any word on how my trip was going, she knew when I was scheduled to leave San Francisco but hadn't heard anything since—and kept calling every day to ask me how things were going and when I was coming out to see them. The truth was I really didn't have time or inclination to talk to her right then, there being no way to describe the situation with one Elliott or another close by; I was busy getting settled in, figuring out the parameters of living with George and Mary Emma under these surprise conditions. Toward the end of the week George and Mary Emma, mainly I think to get away and regroup with a sudden Snodgrass living in their midst, left for a week with friends in New York City over Christmas. I welcomed having the house to myself. But Camille kept calling: "You're going to have to come see us sometime, Dick."

Two days after Christmas, I got in Murray and made the trip to Erieville, wondering if either De or Camille remembered any of the events of my visit last summer, only six months earlier, particularly how De would react to see me again. But if he harbored any ill-will or bad feeling about me, everything was forgotten in De's dance of anger at George. "That son of a bitch! That son of a bitch!" As we sat down to lunch, De asked me to tell them again what happened when I arrived at the Elliotts'. I started the story, doing my best to keep it light—an anecdote amusing for the irony of the situation—but De jumped to his feet and started pacing back and forth behind Camille's chair, fists clenched, the dishes in the china cabinet rattling. "I know what it is," De said with a look of triumph, sitting back down again. "I had a poem published in the *New Yorker* a couple months ago, and George was telling me how he hasn't been able to get anything published lately. That has to be it, he's jealous, and this is his way of getting back at me. That son of a bitch." Camille and I looked at each other across the table but I couldn't read her expression.

Richard Snodgrass

Moving the Hat

After lunch, De said, "Let's take a walk. There's something I want to talk to you about.."

I followed him to the storeroom—as I passed the kitchen, Camille turned from the sink, a concerned look on her face—got our coats and hats and went out the back door into the half-light of the late December afternoon. Where were we going, what did he have in mind? De was following a trail through the snow up the hill toward a half-collapsed barn and several sheds. The Russian and the Cowboy—De in his fur-collared parka and astrachan, me in my sheepskin coat and Stetson—single-file between the drifts in the fields above the house.

What was this about? Did he know what Camille and I talked about on the drive home from the Dikes' party last summer? Did he think there was something going on between us now? I kept a distance between us so I'd have time to react if he whirled around. When we got to one of the sheds he waited for me, then opened the door quickly and pushed me inside, following close behind. The only light came from windows at one corner, though I could make out on the work bench several knives. As I regained my balance I was ready to ward off a blow but then something all wings and claws came swooping down out of the darkness aimed at our heads. I dodged as the owl continued on to the rafters at the other end. "Holy shit!" I said. De laughed. De had volunteered to take care of the wounded bird while it heeled. To feed it, he scooped up road kills into Ziplok bags. Now he opened an ice chest filled with snow, unwrapped a piece of meat, and held it up. The owl lifted from its perch and came swooping down again and grabbed the meat out of De's gloved hand, the wings brushing close to my face as it continued on, taking up a new perch on the crossbeams across the room.

"There's something I want to ask you about Camille," De said.

Here it comes, I thought, get ready.

"Camille needs to know how to work in the darkroom," he said, holding up another piece of meat as the great bird left its perch, "if she's going to take pictures to go along with my poems. Would you be willing to teach her? I'd pay you." *Whoosh!*

Richard Snodgrass

Moving the Hat

The image of the shepherd holding the gate open for the wolf wouldn't be amiss right now. Have at it.

I was disappointed that De wanted Camille to take the photographs for his book of headstone translations; my photographs would be perfect for it, and a book would be a big step in my career. But balanced against that was the prospect of working closely with Camille. Just the two of us. I wasn't sure if I was happy with the idea or scared. Probably some of both. It wasn't De's fault. It was the kind of thing a brother should be able to ask a brother to do. The kind of thing a brother should be able to do with a brother's wife without hesitation or concern. But I knew myself pretty well; I could imagine what could happen between Camille and me. I wondered if Camille was thinking about that too. Eventually, I would wonder how much De did as well.

There was a community darkroom at the University called LightWork. Camille was anxious to get started so I met her there a few days later; it was during the holiday break so there weren't many students around. In a private darkroom, barely room for two people to stand in the aisle between the wet and dry sides, I walked her through the basics of printing, mixing the chemicals, working with the enlarger and the papers, the different baths, washing and finishing the print. Laughing as we brushed up against each other in the narrow confines, me straddling her at times, leaning over against her back as she worked at the sink. In the glow of the safelight, she would turn and look into the side of my face. Smile. As if about to kiss me.

Afterward she said she didn't have to get back right away; we went to a German restaurant and sat side-by-side in a booth drinking dark beer, eating knockwurst. When we left it was snowing again, the snow swirling under the lights from the eaves of the restaurant. Falling and melting on her face. As I held her door for her, she turned and we kissed. "I knew you'd come back for me." "You're the reason I'm here." We kissed again before I helped her into the car and watched her drive away, the taillights absorbed in the swirling snow. And wondered how much of what I said to her was true.

Richard Snodgrass

Moving the Hat

Camille and I continued to meet at the darkroom a couple of days a week—De praised her for her diligence—our passion and lover's explorations continuing until I was ready to hoist her up on the edge of a table or bend her over the print washer. But Camille wanted our first time to be special, so one weekend when De was away giving a reading we packed bags and drove in a snowstorm thirty-five miles south to a motel in Courtland. Unfortunately my ardor and anxiety spoiled our first attempt but we got it right the second. Then realized the snow piling up outside and threat of road closures and slipped and slid back to Erieville. In the guest room bed—we had *some* principles, after all—we picked up where we left off at two in the morning, only to be interrupted by a man's voice at the second-floor window. Panic! De! Murder! No, just a lineman on a ladder making a routine check at this ungodly hour. Sorry, we had a report of a line down in this area. Really? Now, where were we?

When meeting her twice a week wasn't enough, I drove out to Erieville on weekends and Camille and I on some pretext or other went for long drives, parking in turnouts on country roads and climbing in the back of Murray, exposing to the cold just enough skin we imagined like Eskimos. The Elliotts finally left on their European trip and Camille would come to the house on her twice a week schedule; we'd spend long afternoons in the Elliott's double bed, all the windows open to enjoy the warm air washing over our bodies, working our way through an abridged version of the Kama Sutra. Later in the summer De spent several weeks at Yaddo, the writer's colony, and I took up residence at the house in Erieville. After the Elliotts returned, I learned that their neighbors heard our goings-on through those open bedroom windows and they let George know. That came out when I went back to pick up the last of my things and he handed me a bill to refinish a nightstand he said I ruined. When I handed it back to him and suggested furniture polish, he shouted, "You shit on me!" Poor George. I think he was furious that I was doing with Camille what he always wanted to. I left him sputtering under his portico.

Richard Snodgrass

Moving the Hat

I won't hazard a guess as to how much Camille learned about photography during our visits to LightWork, but the directors became acquainted with my work and I was awarded a grant to photograph the mill towns north of Pittsburgh where I grew up, then be artist-in-residence at the darkroom during the month of December. It was fortuitous because the Elliotts were returning at the end of summer, and Camille needed the time on her own to start divorce proceedings, get her own place, and set up a new life for herself.

So come September I journeyed back to my mother's house in Beaver Falls and set up residence in the attic room where I spent my high school years. On gray days, which meant practically every day, the pearl-gray days I remembered growing up here, I would drive to one of the valley towns, set up my view camera, a wooden Deardorff 4x5 named Maggie Mae, and let things happen. My technique was the same as I had used photographing the mining towns in the Sierras; in addition to photographing the mills and the towns, the view camera made me a spectacle that drew people to ask what I was doing, which would often lead to them allowing me to photograph in their houses. At night, with the attic windows covered with heavy cloths, I would sit in total darkness at a card table and develop the sheet film in trays, washing them afterward in the bathroom and drying them on a line in the shower. It was a time of true exploration and discovery, because growing up a nice white Anglo-Saxon (well, okay, Scots-Irish) son of privilege, there were many towns, and even areas in my hometown, I had never been to before, were acquainted with only from a car window, because nice people like Snodgrasses didn't go to places like that. Imagine my surprise.

After Thanksgiving I went back to Syracuse. The LightWork grant included a room in a university dormitory, but I moved in with Camille in her apartment in a house south of the freeway that divided the city. A ground-floor apartment she shared with the black Great Dane Czarny that she had insisted on taking with her to rescue from De's beatings. Because she had little furniture the three of us would sprawl on the floor at night, Czarny a voyeur as Camille and I pursued our passion.

Moving the Hat

I got to the restaurant a good hour before De asked me to meet him there, thinking only in passing of the irony that it was the same restaurant where Camile and I first let our feelings for each other be known. Or was it coincidence? Something more devious? The message De left for me at the darkroom said only "I need to see you." Whatever, I wasn't taking any chances. As I hoped, the bar area was practically empty, Happy Hour just getting started, the dinner crowd not yet begun; there was plenty of time to fix the layout of the restaurant in my mind, figure out the quickest escape routes, places for a possible ambush, locate the side and rear doors where an accomplice could enter. I considered drinking ice water in a rocks glass, pretending it was gin, but wasn't sure I could depend on the bartender to help me carry it off, so I ordered what I was familiar with, Jack Daniels neat with a water back. Something Jack Martin had taught me when we went out drinking after work. "Here's what you do, Dickie, so you never get drunk: you drink one glass of water for every shot of whiskey, and you only drink the good stuff, never the cheap bar shit. Do that and you'll always remain clear." Another thing Jack taught me to do when I was at a bar where things could get ugly, I saved the stool to my left for De; unless my brother had a hell of a backhand, which I was pretty sure he didn't, he'd be cramped in any kind of attack, even with a weapon, I'd have a good chance to block him, and I'd have plenty of room to swing. I couldn't believe it could come to that, De shied away from confrontation, was a physical coward, but you never know, if he had a weapon he might try something out of character. Then I saw him in the mirror behind the bar, threading his way toward me, in his fur-collared double breasted great coat and astrakhan, glistening with snow crystals, his full beard like some storybook wizard.. "Sorry I'm late," he said, getting himself settled. "Camille took the better of our two Saabs, the one with the good tires, and they hadn't plowed beyond Cazenovia." He turned abruptly to look at me. "You do know she left, don't you?"

Richard Snodgrass

Moving the Hat

We made small talk, he asked me how Mother was, how long I'd be in town. Finally he got to it. "Do you know where Camille's living now? Somebody said she has an apartment over on the Southside, but she hasn't seen fit to tell me. Afraid I'll show up, I guess. They also said she's living with some guy. Have you been in touch with her since you've been back—no." He interrupted himself as the bartender brought his drink. I realized he was watching me in the mirror. "No, it's unfair of me to ask you about that. I know you were—are a friend of Camille's too. I can't expect you to simply walk away from your relationship with her just because of what she and I are going through. Any more than I could expect you'd walk away from your relationship with Jan when that marriage ended too. Ha, it seems you've had quite a history of following my trail of broken loves, doesn't it?" He lifted his glass in a toast to the me in the mirror. After more small talk he got to what I realized was his main reason for wanting to see me. "I'm going to ask Mother to loan me the money so I can buy Camille's half of the farm. The property settlement of the divorce will give her half the farm and I want to buy it from her but I don't have that kind of money. Do you think Mother has sixty, seventy thousand left in the trust?" "I have no idea what her financial situation is, I doubt if she'd tell me even if I asked her." I thought a moment. "Seems a bit ironic, doesn't it, you asking her for money? After all you've written about her?" He looked at my reflection. Not friendly. "Well, it has to be. That farm is where I plan to spend my final years, finish my legacy, my Hitler poems. We spend our lives stepping over bodies." He finished his drink, and got ready to leave, a different De. Done with me. "Did I tell you I'm seeing someone? She was a student of mine,: she's not as pretty as Camille but where did pretty get me?" I decided I would leave as well, it would be safer knowing he was gone. Outside it had snowed again, the parking lot was crystalline. We said our good-byes and I headed for my car when he called sharply behind me: "Brother-Man!" He had something in his hand. Aimed at me. Here it comes, I thought. It was a black plastic window scraper. "If you learn anything about Mother's finances, let me know, okay?"

Richard Snodgrass

Moving the Hat

When neither Camille nor Czarny were at the apartment, I followed their tracks through the new-fallen snow. I found her in the next block, a silhouette in the middle of the street; when she saw me, she waved. She had the coal shovel with her that we used on these walks to clean up, leaning on it like a cane. As I approached, Czarny came from between two parked cars, shaking himself after a good shit. "I was so worried," Camille said. "Are you okay? What did he want?" I kissed her upturned face and we did an awkward, shovel-in-one-mittened-hand embrace, her purple quilted parka scrunched against my sheepskin coat. Snowflakes landed on her cold-burned cheeks, lasting for seconds like crystal tears. "Mostly he wanted information about Mother's finances. He wants to hit her up for a loan to buy your half of the farm." "A loan—that's a laugh. We never paid her back for the money she 'loaned' us to buy the farm in the first place. This time he's probably counting on her dying before he has to pay her back." I took the shovel and went over and tried to scoop up the pile of feces in one sweep, a little challenge I gave myself on these walks. "Evidently, he doesn't know a thing about us. He heard you're with someone, but I guess I'm such a non-entity that it's never occurred to him that it could be me." "Don't count on it. It would be like him to act he didn't know anything just to get more information." She turned away and headed back down the street, Czarny trotting alongside her. I followed behind, carrying the pile on the shovel like an offering. Back at her place, while Czarny gave a final sniff-through to the front yard, I went around back to dump the shovel. And wondered, would it always be like this? Would De always be part of the conversation? Wondering what he was up to now, guessing at his motives? Afraid what he'd do next? Czarny didn't seem like the only on-looker in our relationship. When I dumped the fresh shit on the pile it melted a hole for itself in the snow. Around front Camille and the dog were heading toward the front door; she waved, C'mon, Hurry up, a little skip to her step, she had plans for us the rest of the evening. I grinned, hurried up.

Moving the Hat

We thought of moving to Rochester, close enough for Camille's legal battles with De but away from De's immediate orbit. But while I was artist-in-residence at LightWork, the Oakland Museum in California contacted me about a temporary job. While I was on my makeshift MFA program, I contacted the museum and printed some of their historical negatives for them as a special project. They liked my results and now wanted me to print some of Dorthea Lange's early negatives for an upcoming retrospective. Camille and I decided it would probably be best, to get me out of the area; if and when De found out we were lovers he was liable to go ballistic, and it was one more worry and threat she didn't want to go through. It also would fill the time for me before a residence grant I was awarded from the Wurlitzer Foundation in Taos, New Mexico, which began in April. So come the first of the year I loaded up Murray and we set off again, this time retracing our steps back across the country.

In San Francisco, I rented a friend's darkroom to make the Lange prints; and Carol offered to let me camp out on her dining room floor. If she knew about Camille, she didn't say anything though it wouldn't have surprised me if she did, we knew each other very well. She hadn't filed for divorce, partly because she knew I needed to be on her medical insurance, and partly because we both wondered if we might get back together. But the truth was we were best as brother and sister, that was always the most comfortable. We slipped once and tried going to bed together, but it ended with her in tears and me feeling like I had abused a stranger.

A major reason I left San Francisco originally was that I never felt at home there. Returning now, it felt like home and the East Coast was the foreign territory. Go figure. Regardless, when the time came I repacked Murray—Carol wanted no part of good-byes; she hoped I was gone before she got home from work—and set out once again, following the trail to New Mexico, arriving in Taos on Holy Saturday. Easter morning I went for a walk into town where the spirits of the place told me this new world went beyond adobe architecture and exposed vigas and blue-black mountains under mounting skies.

Richard Snodgrass

Moving the Hat

"Bet you won't be wearing that hat in the Southwest," the unabashedly gay salesclerk said, rather cattily, in the Union Square men's shop when he heard where I was headed. The hat he referred to was the Great Feathered Stetson, a straw model I wore in hot weather to which I had added a hawk feather I found along the highway stuck flamboyantly in the headband. I thought I understood what the salesman meant when I got to Taos and saw all the tourists walking around wearing Western hats, cowboy for a day. It was enough to make me leave my Stetson in the closet except I had been wearing a hat for several years now, feather or no, it was a part of me.

Beyond keeping your head warm or dry, a hat can be an announcement, a declaration, a demonstration that the person wearing it is special or at least considers themselves so. Want to indicate a leader, royalty, a priest? Give that person a headpiece. It can be a symbol of belonging, a member of the tribe, one of us. It can also be self-aggrandizing, presumptuous, pretentious. I encountered the darker meanings of a hat when one Sunday afternoon at a gallery opening I walked into a fight starting among half a dozen guys who had too much champagne. On jobsites I broke up fights several times, but I discovered it was far more dangerous trying to be a peacemaker when you didn't wear the white hat of an inspector. One guy with a tangly beard and built like a linemaker singled me out. "I want a piece of you." Whoa! Not my intention on a Sunday afternoon. I raised my hands, ducked my head, no contest, and tried to slip away to another room but the guy followed me, reptilian, calling me back. In the main room I lost him finally in the crowd and confusion, out into the sunlight. But I was shaken. I walked around the plaza for a while, then returned to the gallery, trying to piece together what had happened. The guy who had been after me was outside with his wife or girlfriend; trying to smooth things over, I approached him to ask if he was okay. Stupid. As soon as he saw me he flew into a rage again, it was all the woman could do to restrain him. "Please, just get out of here. It's your hat."

Richard Snodgrass

Moving the Hat

If ever there was a place where the name Snodgrass held no sway, not even as an amusement, it was Taos and Northern New Mexico. Sway? The name there was so removed from the prevailing culture that it couldn't even be funny. For the first time in my life I was the minority; I was an Anglo in local terminology, and it wasn't a term of endearment. Hispanics were the majority, though they were adamant that they were Spanish, descendants of conquistadors from the 16th Century; they were not to be confused with Mexican-Americans who arrived after the Mexican–American War and the Mexican Revolution, and they absolutely weren't Chicanos. When I first arrived at the Foundation, I asked Freddie, the Spanish caretaker, about a certain bar I had seen; he looked horrified: "Oh Deeck, you mustn't go there, you are so tall, and so white!" The area was the most violent place where I had ever lived. Shootings, fire-bombing tourists cars, attacks and beatings were a daily occurrence, pistols displayed on restaurant tabletops. It was said Frank Shorter, the Olympic runner, there for training, was once confronted on a desert road by several men for nothing more than he was white; a marathon runner, Shorter quickly outpaced his assailants, but still. . . . In driving between Taos and Santa Fe, I was instructed to avoid the very Spanish town of Española, if I had car trouble I should push it clear of the city limits rather than be caught there. An exaggeration, no doubt, there are undoubtedly good and kindly folk in Española, but none of the Anglos I knew tempted it.

The Land of Enchantment, according to the State motto. Well, there is certainly something going on there. As if to balance the violence in the air, there were the spirits of the place, the undeniable presence of something Other. Hmm, there's that plus-minus thing again. Science tells us of different planes of existence, four dimensions, five dimensions. Somewhere Castaneda has Don Juan talk of sorcerers handling seven dimensions, with awareness of many more; String Theory posits ten dimensions; Buddhism talks of thirty-one planes of existence, etc. Whatever. I don't blame you if you're dubious, but spend time in northern New Mexico and you definitely get the sense that there are things going on around us beyond our comprehension.

Oh yes, and then there are the Indians.

Richard Snodgrass

Moving the Hat

From the time I arrived at the Wurlitzer I was told I had to see an Indian dance, so I drove to San Felipe pueblo for their Feast Day. My idea of an Indian dance pretty much coincided with my brother's poem "Pow-Wow," which described a sad affair with men doing shuffling dances they've seen in movies to recreate their tribe's past glories. I found my way to a central plaza inside the stacked stucco buildings where people were gathering, Indians and a few Anglos, sitting on the ground or household chairs around the perimeter. I took a seat on the ground but just to make sure I asked an old man seated in a chair behind me if I was okay where I was. He laughed a little and motioned for me to turn around. A few minutes later he leaned forward and said, "What you will see here today is very sacred." He nodded for emphasis then looked away.

With the perimeter filled with people, half a dozen men in white pants and colorful solid-colored shirts took a position in the center of the plaza with a tall drum. The drum began a slow steady beat and the men began to chant as the dancers entered the plaza following a tall banner, two files, side-by-side, alternating two men and two women, hundreds of them of all ages, the men in white dance kilts, with turtleshell rattles and bells tied to their legs, each carrying a pine bough in one hand a gourd rattle in the other, the women in long black dresses carrying pine boughs as well. The men danced like a slow running in place, the women's feet patting the ground, as they circled the plaza slowly, half a dozen sacred clowns painted in black and white stripes shouting encouragement. The files of dancers circled the plaza weaving in and out for nearly an hour before leaving and I thought that was that, but then another group entered from the other end, doing the same dance. At one point the old man learned forward and said, "There are dancers and there are watchers. But some dancers are only watching, and some watchers are actually dancing." I looked at him but he acted like he hadn't said anything, so I turned back around. When the dancing was over several hours later I turned around to ask him what he meant but there was no one there.

Richard Snodgrass

Moving the Hat

I was at the Wurlitzer to work on a novel that, thirty-five years later, I published entitled *The Pattern Maker*. But in the days following my visit to San Felipe pueblo I was haunted by the question: Why were all those people dancing? I put the novel aside and started to read everything I could about pueblo Indians, as well as attending dances at pueblos from Taos to Zuni. Which led me to the kachina dances of the Hopi. Kachinas are spiritual messengers from the gods who visit the Hopi pueblos six months of the year; the word also refers to the dancers who become the kachina when they put on the kachina mask; as well as the kachina dolls carved to instruct children. I once read a story by Evan S. Connell about a man who, if I recall correctly (don't count on it) finds a condor in his suburban backyard that soon becomes the centerpiece of cocktail parties and barbeques; the huge bird puts up with it all until it spreads its wings and flies away. And I got an idea: suppose a man found a kachina in his backyard, how would he react, why would the kachina be there? The novel, *There's Something in the Back Yard*, soon took over my life, all my struggles to find my voice in my fiction came naturally now as I worked on the book. I worked around the clock, two hours on, two hours off, fueled by strong coffee, the same schedule I had in Syracuse only now with tapes of Linda Ronstadt and Jackson Browne. The director at the Foundation was so impressed with my work ethic that he offered me extensions to my original grant; all told I spent 18 months in Taos. When I left I traveled to the Hopi reservation in northern Arizona for the Home dances where the kachinas say good-by to the pueblos before returning to their home in the San Francisco mountains. I camped out under a juniper tree for a month, living out of the back end of Murray, spending the days when there weren't dances sitting at a picnic table beside the Hopi Cultural Center rereading John Gardner's *The Sunlight Dialogues* and writing the book within my book, *Retold Tales of the Hopi*. When I finally left Hopi, I got as far as Flagstaff before collapsing in a motel, barely able to get out of bed for four days.

Richard Snodgrass

Moving the Hat

"So, what was Carmen doing all this time?"

"You mean Camille?"

"Whatever."

Marty is proud of her little dig.

My relationship with Camille had been reduced to passionate letters while she got her affairs in Syracuse in order; a job as an assistant at the Everson Museum of Art convincing her that she wanted to be a chef. At Christmas time she visited me for a week; when we finally got out of bed on Christmas eve, I took her to midnight Mass at Santo Domingo pueblo, said to be the most traditional of the New Mexico pueblos, the only time in the year that they danced within the church. Later she said it was a great awakening for her; unfortunately it was an awakening for me as well. The pews had been removed from the church; we stood against the side wall, the church crowded with people from the pueblo and a scattering of Anglos. Long after midnight, a distant drum announced the arrival of the dancers; the doors burst open and in came two files of men advancing up the aisle toward the altar, deer dancers, antlers on their heads, bodies painted white above their dance kilts, the jingling of the small bells tied to their legs filling the church along with the drum and the chant of the singers, two Koshares dancing between the files. Then they were gone, the drum and the jingling bells fading into the night. As we went back to the car Camille looked spellbound. "I've waited all my life for this," she said. Uh-oh.

A few months later she moved to Santa Fe, to be closer to me and her newly discovered love of Indian culture. The locals called them White Indians, Anglos so enamored of Indians that they embraced their culture in place of their own. You would see them in towns and at dances, dripping with turquoise and squash blossom jewelry, linen shirts decorated with eagles and lightning bolts and kokopelli, the women in moccasins and buckskin skirts. Watching Camille's transformation was like watching a drug addict spiraling downward. My own awakening came when I went to see *The Deer Hunter*. So much of the Vietnam sections of the movie were simply wrong, but I stayed twice to see the scenes of the Western Pennsylvania mill town. My culture. I continued to go to dances, to Hopi, but always one-step removed, aware I didn't belong there, an observer but not a participant, dancing but not dancing.

Richard Snodgrass

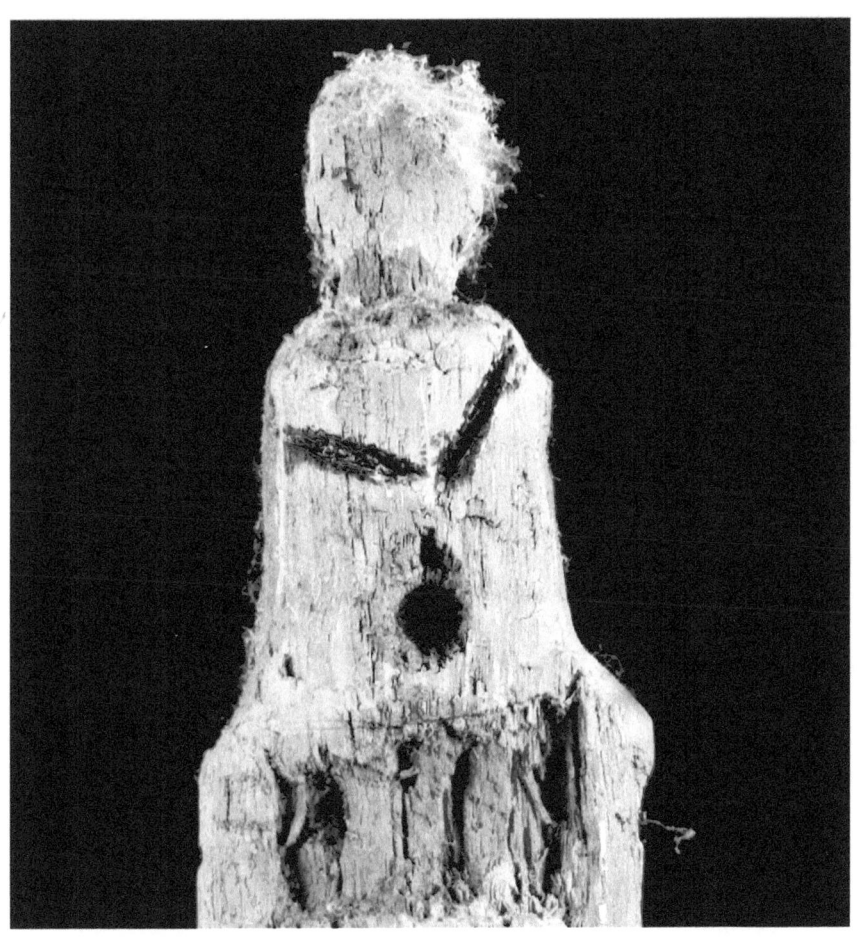

Moving the Hat

After Hopi, I went back to San Francisco to do a freelance job writing a brochure for a testing lab, camped out once again on Carol's floor. After the turmoil of the last couple of years, the pinballing from free place to free place, it was comfortable being with her again, maybe that was enough. Things were complicated, however, because I had agreed to meet Camille in Gallup in early December to go to Shalako at Zuni pueblo. At Shalako half a dozen or so ten-foot-tall bird-like creatures come to the pueblo and dance all night in houses specially prepared for them. I didn't want to leave my stuff with Carol, taking up space in her apartment, so I loaded up Murray and was on the road again. The two nights I was traveling, I called Carol from my motel and we chatted like an old married couple, which in fact we were. But all ideas of settling washed away when I saw Camille in Gallup; we spent the afternoon in bed before heading out for Zuni in her rental car.

We stayed at the ceremony only a few hours, anxious to get back to the motel. In the morning, after putting it off as long as possible, I followed in Murray as she drove back to Albuquerque to catch her plane to Poughkeepsie where she had started classes at the Culinary Institute of America. And I couldn't stand the thought of being away from her, the feel of her body, her flesh. I was balanced on my own continental divide; from here I could go west, back to what was known, I could probably get a job as an inspector, be with Carol; or there was east, the unknown, I could figure some way to keep writing, keep chasing my art, be with Camille. Sitting in the airport restaurant with her, I blurted out, "I could come to Poughkeepsie." "I thought you were going back to San Francisco?" "There's nothing for me there, that was then, this is now." Her face broke into tears of joy. We made plans; I had all my things with me, I would drive to Poughkeepsie and join her there. More tears, joy. Then she was gone, away in a silver bird. I went back to Murray and followed the signs to East Interstate 40, scanning the radio for Linda Ronstadt singing "Hasten Down the Wind" or Jennifer Warnes' "Shot Through the Heart."

Richard Snodgrass

Moving the Hat

Camille's apartment was in Hyde Park, outside of Poughkeepsie, in a complex of multi-storied motel-style apartment buildings in a forest setting. She still had little furniture; a previous tenant left a large spool used for telephone cables that was her dining table, chairs were upturned crates cushioned with folded blankets. For the first few weeks the regular passionate sex covered a multitude of doubts but reality was beginning to set in for me. I tried to work on *There's Something in the Back Yard* through the days, sitting at the cable spool, while she was at class but I felt more distant from the Hopi mesas than the actual twenty-five hundred miles. And I was no help to Camille. She was having trouble at the school, not with the classes but with male-dominated kitchen culture; she was one of the few women and was the subject of endless bullying and lewd remarks. Also, something she didn't tell me in Albuquerque was that the apartment cost more than she could afford and she was hoping I would join her to split the rent and utilities. My unemployment was finally coming to an end, the money from freelance writing jobs was dwindling fast, my main resource was food stamps; I hated myself for it but I resented being committed to a place that I had never chosen for myself. Camille kept suggesting that I could get a job, bring in some more money, a legitimate request on her part, but I felt I was being buried alive.

And there was endless talk of De. His latest maneuvering in the divorce, what he was up to now, what he might do next. I admitted to myself what I suspected earlier, that he would always be part of my relationship with Camille, there would always be three of us. I would never be able to look at her without seeing him. I hated myself for it but I had to get away. One of the most dishonorable things I had ever done in my life. When Mother mentioned in a phone call that there had been break-ins at the house, I told Camille I was going to Beaver Falls for a few months to help my mother, I would be coming back but I'd take my stuff with me so I could keep working on my book, don't worry, don't cry, it's only for a little while. As I drove away her image was framed briefly in Murray's sideview mirror, waving and waving, then was gone among the trees.

Richard Snodgrass

Moving the Hat

So there I was, 40 years-old and living in my mother's attic, this time outfitted with a hotplate and makeshift refrigerator, both to give myself some degree of autonomy and because it looked like I was going to be there for a while. I tried not to compare myself to Stewie Hammerle who was living with his mother at the other end of the block, his gypo flatbed semi taking up half the parking on the street. I told myself I had no real alternative if I wanted to keep writing; and my mother actually needed help, half a dozen times I confronted someone trying to break into the house one way or another, her stories of waking up from a nap to find "some man" proved to be true. To justify my situation to myself, I doubled down on my writing schedule, two hours on, two hours off, around the clock, often running into my mother in the kitchen in the middle of the night when I snuck down for something, she had always been a night-owl. I also took advantage of the isolation to do the reading I had always intended to. I had grown up hearing the bells of McCartney Library at the college a block away sounding the half hour but I had never been in the place. One day I took a walk and found that local residents had full privileges to the library. And what a collection. Sitting on my bed I went through the complete works of Faulkner, Hemingway, Fitzgerald, Henry James, then a real find, James Froude's four-volume biography of Thomas Carlysle. Among my other reading I began a study of English prose styles, trying to find the antecedents of where my own style was heading, prompted by a book given to me by the poet John Balaban who I met at the Wurlitzer. I discovered my affinity to what Cyril Connolly called, as opposed to the Plain Style, the Mandarin style. "The Mandarin style at its best yields the richest and most complex expression of the English language. . . . It is characterized by long sentences with many dependent clauses, by the use of the subjunctive and conditional, by exclamations and interjections, quotations, allusions, metaphors, long images. . .subtlety and conceits. Its cardinal assumption is that neither the writer nor the reader is in a hurry. . . ." (Enemies of Promise, London, 1938)

Yep, sounded about right.

Richard Snodgrass

Moving the Hat

"Let me see if I've got this right, Snots. You came back here to finish a novel you're writing about Indians, and then you want to write about life in mill towns."

"And to help my mother."

"Yeah, right. Help Mama Snots. Okay, I get the part about writing a novel about Indians, that could be interesting if you like Indians, which I don't especially. But why would you want to write about life in a mill town? That sure as hell doesn't sound interesting to me, but maybe it's different when you're living it."

Ted and I are sitting in a bar in Pittsburgh's university district having a beer before we head back to Beaver Falls. I know Ted—who works ten-hour days, six days a week at the Tube Mill—well enough not to try to explain. Ted Krzemienski was my best friend in high school, the only person besides family I saw on my trips home. Since I've been back, every Saturday I'm expected to watch college football games at his apartment while his wife Marilyn fills me with snacks so I won't have to worry about dinner, the same on Sunday with the pro games. Ted was the only person in town when my father died to go to the interment, his rattly old Chevy trailing the cortege of funeral home Cadillacs. When Ted found out that I come occasionally to the university district in Pittsburgh, he asked to join me; I told him that all I do is some photocopying and go to the museum, but he wants to see for himself, he's sure I have a girl here. I only wish. He waited for me at Kinko's and followed along while I went to the Carnegie. I always visit certain paintings—the Bonnard's, the Cezannes, Monet's Water Lillies, the Francis Bacon—but I was afraid he'd be bored so I took him to the Dinosaur Hall. He looked at the skeletons, touched the 38-million-year-old femur, and declared, "It's interesting, but you know these aren't real, don't you? No way."

Now Ted says as he drains his Iron City, "One thing, brother. You're not going to keep wearing that cowboy hat, are you?"

"Technically, it's more of a fedora...."

"I don't care if it's your Aunt Millie. It makes you look like a turkey."

"Sorry, it's my hat."

Ted slips off his stool and heads for the door, muttering as only Ted can, "Fucking turkey."

Moving the Hat

I stayed sequestered most of the time in the attic, only seeing my mother in passing, on my way some place or other, rarely saying anything more than hello or goodbye, never spending time downstairs with her. But even that brief contact was enough to do me in. All the good feelings I had about her, all the things I had learned about her that helped me realize her side of the family's stories, realize that she was a person with hopes and fears and regrets and wishes all of her own—all I had learned to overcome the indoctrination of my brother—disappeared in my desperation of living back in the house at the age of forty, the fear that all that I had done and achieved in my life, my life in San Francisco, came to nothing, that I was a nothing. All my mother had to do as I passed her was to ask if I wanted something to eat, to make the most inane comment about the weather or how the Steelers were doing, and I flew into an inner, and sometimes not so inner, rage. I finally accepted that I needed help and made the call to Beaver County Social Services. A very calm young woman on the other end of the line said Yes, they could certainly help me, and asked if I was in danger of hurting myself. I said no, I was afraid I was about to kill my mother. They set me up with an appointment the next day.

I couldn't imagine I'd find a first-rate therapist in this intellectual backwater; after all, I was experienced with some of the best—read: I was special—I had been in therapy at UC Berkeley: So there! I was assigned a woman about my own age named Jane, tall, blonde, statuesque. Oh dear. This could be trouble, knowing my tendencies around attractive women. To get me through the crisis, she set up appointments several times a week. In my best therapy mode, I would launch into detailed recountings of my dreams; she would smile benevolently, shake her head, and say, "That's all very interesting, but what did you eat today? Did you get your car tuned up? What about seeing a dentist for that tooth?" Jane pulled me out of my self-indulgent Freudian labyrinths to face the fact that all the introspection in the world doesn't mean a thing if you can't negotiate the mundane realities of the everyday. As for my being attracted to her, she made me confront that reality too: "That's very flattering, Richard, but don't concern yourself. In your current situation, you could never afford me."

Richard Snodgrass

Moving the Hat

I don't remember where I had been that day, Pittsburgh most likely, but it was late when I got back to the house, after eleven, though as always every light was on; Mother wasn't at her usual station, sitting at her cardtable in the living room sorting through papers of one kind or another. I thought she must have gone to bed, so I went foraging for snacks. I was midway through the narrow pantry between the dining room and kitchen when I met her coming the other direction.

"Hello there, my sweet patootie, can I get you something to eat?"

It was the last thing I needed, her gray-haired jocularity, after a disappointing day. I tried to move around her, get by her, but when I moved left she moved right, when I moved right she moved left, the two of us doing a little dance.

"I have some leftover ham, and there's oranges and apples, I could make you some toast."

In my mind's eye I saw the contents of the refrigerator, months'-old Tupperware cloudy with seven layers of mold. She looked at me through her bottle lenses, twiddled her fingers, raised on her toes good-naturedly. I lost it. All my frustrations, all my disappointments, seemed to be standing there in front of me, blocking my way, mocking me. In a total rage I grabbed a broom handle leaning against the wall—what the hell was a spare broom handle doing there anyway?—and gripped it like a baseball bat, ready to swing.

"Are you going to hit me with that?" she asked. Calmly, as if not surprised in the least.

And then a wondrous thing happened. Jane and I had been discussing lately the scripts personal relations fall into, like tape recordings made years ago that we keep mindlessly repeating, recreating old dialogues written years before. And it occurred to me: Wait a minute! This is an old script, and I didn't even write it, that was my brother. How about we change the tape.

"I was thinking of it," I told her, then put the handle down. "But why don't we try something different. Let's do a hug."

I held out my arms and she walked into them, resting her head on my chest. I realized she was crying. "It's been thirty years since anybody held me."

It was the start of a beautiful friendship. Imagine my surprise.

Richard Snodgrass

Moving the Hat

The problem with being alone a lot, I found, is that you forget how to be with people; the prospect of a coming interaction—shopping at the supermarket, getting the car serviced, going to the laundromat—could take on monstrous proportions, keep me awake for days ahead of time. The bank was the hardest. The checks from selling my cameras had to be cashed; food stamps collected; cash advances made from my credit cards. All required facing a teller, explaining my situation, trying to bank (heh heh) on the Snodgrass name, the fact my family had dealt there for generations. Before entering, I'd have to jack myself up, give myself a pep talk, you can do this, it's only a big deal if you make it a big deal, put on your inspector's persona, watch out, world, her I come. I'd walk through the door and make my way down the teller line looking for what I hoped was a friendly face. Every time I could, I chose a young woman named Marty.

"Isn't this fun?" I'd say, falling back on my San Francisco patter, making a joke out of the situation, trying for a smile. "We're playing bank."

Marty looked at me like I was a Martian. "Who's playing? This is my job. Do you want a roll of quarters again for the laundromat?"

Well, so much for the old routines.

Then I realized she was Ted's downstairs neighbor, she and her husband living on the first floor of the house. I also realized she was often about when I was there, sweeping the porch when I arrived, raking leaves when I left. It began to seem more than a coincidence.

"She's married, Snots, forget it."

"All I said was you never see her husband. . . ."

"Ain't got nothing to do with you, son. No way no how."

She was the prettiest and the nicest young woman in town, tall and willowy, with reddish curly hair and an open smile. But Ted needn't have worried. For one thing I had had enough of involvement with other people's marriages; for another, she was at least a dozen years younger than I was. No, I wasn't going to tie myself in knots again after I just got untangled .

*

"It's about time," Marty says now, looking over my shoulder at the computer screen. "I was wondering when you'd get to the juicy part."

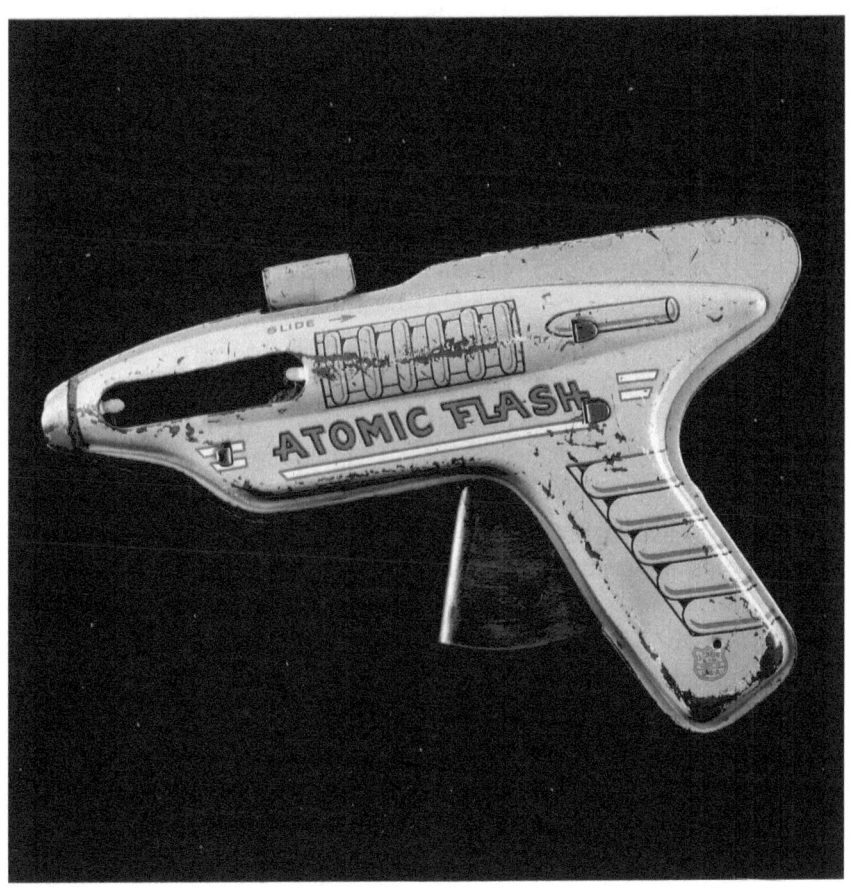

Moving the Hat

Then one evening I was sitting at my desk in the attic when I heard from the open dormer window, "Hello? Hello?" Hard to believe anyone would be calling to me, but I got up and went to the window. There, down in the street standing beside her car, was Marty. When she saw me, she held up a white paper bag in each hand. "I was beginning to think you weren't home. I brought you a sandwich and some ice cream but you better hurry, the ice cream is starting to melt."

She said Ted told her about my living in my mother's attic; and that afternoon a guy came into the bank selling hoagies and she thought I might like one. Then she thought I should have ice cream to go with it, chocolate marshmallow from Waite's, her favorite, but she didn't figure on it melting so fast. When I asked her how she knew where I lived, she said, "Oh, everyone knows the Snodgrass house. And I went to Geneva, I used to walk by here all the time. But you better hurry and get this inside before it's chocolate marshmallow soup."

What just happened here? I wondered if Ted put her up to it but no, she said it was her own idea when I asked her about it at the bank the following week. As was her idea to ask me down for coffee the following Saturday morning. I thought she must mean coffee with her and her husband, which I wasn't looking forward to at all, but it turned out to be just her. Seems her husband was away on Saturday mornings at what he said was barbershop quartet practice (A barbershop quartet? Lord...) though she found out later he was actually visiting a girlfriend in Ellwood City. My visit to her apartment that morning started a series of Saturday mornings coffee klatches, followed by her invitation to dinners, again with just her—more rehearsals supposedly—Friday nights after she got off work at 8 o'clock. Marty had the idea that she could be friends with a guy without any sexual involvement; she gave that up several months later when she discovered you could have sexual feelings with someone you were friends with. For once I took it very slow, I had been seeing her more than six months before we even kissed. There was always so much to talk about. . . .

Richard Snodgrass

Moving the Hat

In time Marty began visiting me for overnights in the attic. I would distract my mother as she sat in the living room at her card table sorting papers, walking around her so she faced away from the front hall as Marty tip-toed by and up the stairs. On weekends, when my mother went to church, we snuck down for showers. It was winter and there was no heat in the attic; my mother kept the downstairs at sweltering levels and I depended on it traveling up the stairs. One day when I was passing through my mother asked me, "Are you warm enough up there?" I told her I was. Then she said, "Is Marty?" After that we didn't hide Marty's visits, she and my mother would have little chats before we went up to my room; I had forgotten this was the woman who shacked up in Chicago for a week with my dad before they were married. Marty and my mother discovered there were long-standing connections between the two families. Marty's great-grandfather, a wealthy industrialist in town, was best friends with my grandfather, Doc Snodgrass; when the family brought my mother back to Beaver Falls to live with them, to celebrate the first night they took the young couple to Doc's best friend's house for dinner. A house a block away on the college campus that was an orange-brick twin to our own. Plus Marty's mom had gone to Geneva with my sister Barbara. No wonder we felt as if we had known each other forever, in certain ways we had.

Marty had kicked her husband out of the house and was filing for divorce. Without her husband around I spent more time at her place, though that got complicated because her former in-laws lived in sight a block away. I expected blow-back from her immediate neighbors, but it turned out they all thought her husband was a shit and welcomed me for making Marty happy. Even Ted, begrudgingly.

"I'll tell you, Snots, I think you're an immoral son-of-a-bitch," he told me one night in the kitchen. "But anyone who tries to get to you has got to go through me first, and don't you forget it. And if you want to run away to get married, I'll ride shotgun, just in case. Brother." When we did get married a year later, Ted was best man, after getting totally lost trying to find the church, you turkey.

Richard Snodgrass

Moving the Hat

After I was in the house for a year or so, my sister Shirley wanted to have a family celebration for Mother's eightieth birthday; the problem was that De said he wouldn't come if I was there. Sigh. Mother said if he was going to be that way about it he shouldn't come, but I knew how much it would mean to her to have De there. I told her I'd vacate the place for a couple days and then she could tell me about the party when I got back, that way she could experience it all over again. De finally agreed but sent word through his son, Russell, that I better not renege because he swore he would kill me on sight. Spoil sport. I sent back that if he was going to try it he better be good because he'd only have one chance. Happy Birthday, Mom.

He wrote about the visit in *After-Images: Autobiographical Sketches* though what he said was mainly fiction of sorts. He wrote that he brought along a ceremonial kris in case I didn't keep my promise to stay away. Really? If I was going to a knife-fight, the last thing I would take is a ceremonial anything. No, I don't think Mother gave him scoldings because she thought there was something improper going on between me and Camille; from what she told me her only surprise was that it hadn't happened earlier, she had noticed the way we looked at each other. True, De slept in Barbara's bed, but that was on the second floor, not in my locked attic room. No, I didn't leave typescripts of my unfinished novels with which I intended to eclipse his work beside his bed; one of the last things I wanted at this stage of our relationship was for him to see my work of any kind. No, I did not leave on my desk a stack of love letters from Camille that I hoped he would read; I had destroyed all my letters from Camille months earlier. No, I never revealed my affair with Camille to his daughter Cynthia; Cynthia had never been a confidant. De needed an enemy, a villain, somebody out to get him, in order to do his best work. He was a man in a bunker looking out at those trying to do him in. Poet as counter-puncher. And who better than a betraying brother. It was colorful, epic, Biblical even; sounded so good in interviews. Glad to oblige.

Richard Snodgrass

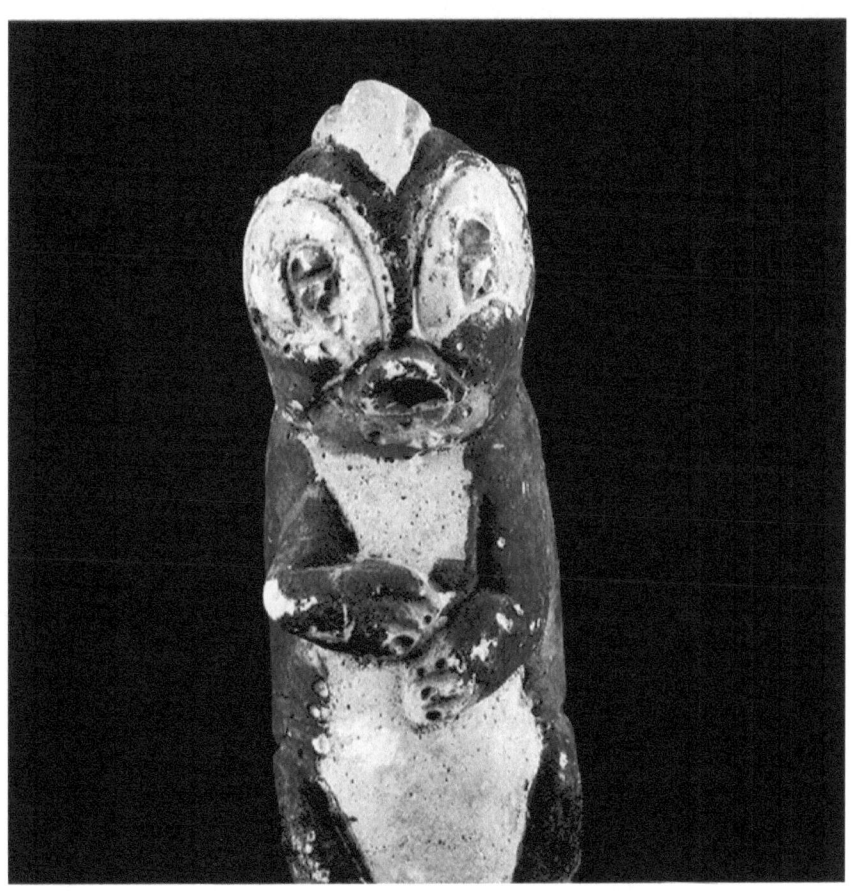

Moving the Hat

It was a morning a few months later when I came down to the second floor to the bathroom and found feces on the hallway rug. I cleaned it up and hoped it was an isolated incident. But a few mornings later when I came down I realized that Mother was still in bed. I looked in on her and asked if she was okay. Her response was garbled, her face wouldn't work right, and I called Shirley who lived across town and who was her primary caregiver. We decided that things were out of our hands now and I called for an ambulance. The EMS technician, a black woman the size of two regular women, took one look at Mother, picked her up in her arms like a baby and carried her down the stairs and the front steps to a waiting gurney. At the hospital they confirmed it was a stroke and diagnosed that she would be incapacitated the rest of her life. Outside her room I asked the doctor how long she might go on like this. "Oh, she could go on for years, she's a strong piece of protoplasm, who knows what will finally finish her off."

Thus started the terrible balancing act of what Mother needed to sustain her and how much her finances could afford. Eventually they bounced her out of the hospital, saying hers was no longer a medical problem, it was a maintenance problem. They might as well have said a warehousing problem. Shirley and I did a hurried tour of available facilities, she and her husband Rusty handled the finances, I never knew what we were working with. At one point the only place I could find was in Steubenville, Ohio. I travelled there and found her lying on a cot with her gown scrunched up under her arms and no blanket; I got that rectified at least for a while. We finally located her at a place in the country outside Ellwood City, a farmhouse with beds squeezed in like rip-rap, a dozen to a room. The first time I visited her there she cried in my arms. She soon found her own solution: she stopped eating. It was only a few weeks later that I got the call that she was dead. And that was that. De didn't come to the funeral and why would he? An empty gesture at this point that wouldn't serve anyone.

Richard Snodgrass

Moving the Hat

Which left the house to be cleaned out. Forty-some years' worth of stuff, gathered by a woman who rarely met stuff she didn't like. Shirley begged off, understandably so with her own family to take care of, so that left me. I was living downstreet with Marty by this time, so every morning, after walking her to her job at the bank, I would drive to the Big House and start my day filling black garbage bags. It took nearly a month and I filled more than 300 before I was through; most satisfying of all was opening a window on the second or third floor and pitching them out, hoping they didn't burst when they landed. At night I would take the day's finds down to Marty's—vintage kitchen implements, a miniature hand wringer meant for gloves, antique toys. In a back closet behind my bed—as a child I was told it opened to a secret staircase to the basement; this was the first time in my life I dared open it—I found a box of my grandfather's stock certificates; I gave them to Rusty, thinking our fortune was made, but he said they were worthless and I never saw them again. I've always wondered. . . . In a bookcase in the living room I found a dozen first editions of Heart's Needle which I sent to De a few years later as a peace offering, suggesting that we talk about what happened with Camille to clear the air but he politely refused. Which was understandable, and probably for the best. Why would I even suggest such a thing? And in Mother's secretary I found a note that she wrote to De but never sent that indicated despite his use of pseudonyms she was aware of the hurtful poems he wrote about her.

> I read your poems and my heart broke again - that I had failed so badly and so often failed when you most needed a mother who could listen, understand and by hearing yourself you might talk out some of the problems, perhaps help yourself find an answer to some of the questions and problems. It's too late by years now - you have fought through the problems and not are the brilliant man you were meant to be and a wonderful father to your children

Richard Snodgrass

```
                        W. D. Snodgrass
                        308 Delaware Circle
                        Newark, DE, 19711

                        March 18, 1988
```

Dear Dick,

Thank you for the copies of Heart's Needle which I can indeed use for friends, and for the nice things you said about my work. Naturally, I hope you're right.

I am grateful, too, for many of the things you said about what happened between you, Camille and myself -- though you can imagine that I see those events very differently. In any case, I appreciate what you said about the pain involved and much of what you said seems to me manly and honest.

I confess that I'm not quite certain of the intentions of your letter. I think its purpose was self-fulfilling -- that you hoped to feel better, having sent such a letter. You don't suggest that we should try to re-establish our relationship; that seems wise to me. I don't see that anything could be gained and a great deal could be lost by any such effort.

I don't say this with intent to wound, only to define what seems wiser to me. If, however, this makes you feel sorry to have sent the books, please drop a postcard and I'll be glad to send them back.

Meantime, I hope that your work is going well and that your life is progressing much as you'd want it to.

                        Sincerely,

Moving the Hat

Marty and I lived in Beaver Falls for a couple of years, until we realized we were spending every weekend and a lot of weeknights running up to Pittsburgh for shows or movies or concerts. At the same time it was becoming apparent to Marty as well as to the powers-that-be at the bank that she was meant for other things than counting money and issuing food stamps. She was encouraged to apply for a job in the main office in Pittsburgh and they quickly scooped her up to be a procedures writer in corporate operations. We took the opportunity to move to Bellevue, a twelve-minute drive or half-hour bus ride from the Golden Triangle. Most days I drove her to work and picked her up again afterward, sometimes even for lunch. As for me, my mother had left me a small inheritance, and we parceled it out to pay half our expenses so I could keep writing full-time. It was also my responsibility to take care of most of the household chores, laundry, grocery shopping with our $30-a-week budget, cooking pots of stew and soup. Meanwhile, Marty's promotions were coming fast as she realized her potential and came into her own, morphing into a procedures training specialist and then project leader for acquisitions and such. I was awarded a grant from the Pennsylvania Council on the Arts that kept us afloat a bit longer, but my money was running out and I needed to get a job, at least part-time. I couldn't stomach the thought of being a construction inspector again, but I reasoned I certainly knew how to write. Well, why not a copywriter for an ad or public relations agency? I sent out my resumes—I didn't know the first thing about copywriting but found textbooks at the Pitt bookstore—and damn if I didn't get some interviews. I owned up that I had no specific experience in the field, but that I was confident I could write anything that was thrown at me—give me a half hour reading your files and I'd write a document that you couldn't tell if you wrote it or not. The guy who hired me said later he did so to prove me wrong. It also didn't hurt that he had known my sister Shirley at Thiel College, that Snodgrass-name thing again—

"Wait a minute, wait a minute!" Marty interrupts. "What do you think you're doing?"

Richard Snodgrass

"Where are you going with this? It sounds like you're turning this book into a work history, me at the bank and you at the ad agency, and that would be as dry as—"

"I know: stale toast," I offer. "That's what you said earlier. . . ."

"I did?"

"You did."

"If you say so," which means she doesn't believe me for a second. Marty's memory is selective; I'm told at work she could remember every ATM screen from five years earlier; but she's not always sure of the date we got married. It's important that a husband not make too much of a thing like that.

"The last thing you want to do," she goes on, "if I understand what you set out to do in the first place, is to finish this book with your time at the ad agency. Yes, that might be interesting in another context, it was quirky with a lot of weird characters and unforeseen twists. And there were plenty of people at that agency who thought you'd fail, who wanted you to fail, and you proved them wrong, you carved out a place for yourself and beat them at their own game. But the thing is, you set out in this book to talk about your lifelong journey to find yourself as an artist, to find your voice in your art, moving your hat around until you found the place to take your stand, which ironically enough was right back where you started, and with a woman," she curtsies, "who was more or less with you, in genetic structure if not in bodily presence, from the beginning. You produced a body of work to be proud of—"

"If little known."

She ignores me. "And you did it—get ready for it, we're going to tie it all together—by maintaining your balance between your work and a job. A feat of skill and daring. . . ," she demonstrates by walking, with much arm waving against the supposed pull of gravity, along an invisible tightrope across the living room floor, executing a pirouette at the midpoint before proceeding to a safe landing on the other side. She turns and takes an open-armed bow. ". . .that's a testament to your drive and your passion. That's what the rest of your book should be about."

Lord, it's tough to live with when she's right. Again. She would say *still*.

Richard Snodgrass

Moving the Hat

While I was still living in my mother's attic, I finished my novel about the Hopi, *There's Something in the Back Yard*, and sent it off to my five most-desired publishers, aware that without representation it would probably end up in a slush pile. Still, I thought I'd take a chance; George Elliott, in happier times, once asked his agent, Georges Borchardt, about how I could get an agent; Borchardt replied, "He can't get an agent without a book published, and he can't get a book published without an agent." Not very encouraging. Then in a stroke of serendipity, blind fate, other worldly intervention, O Fortuna, whatever—Larry Woiwode, author of *What I'm Going to Do, I Think* and *Beyond the Bedroom Wall*, recent books I very much admired, a currant darling of the literary establishment, turned up for a brief residency at Geneva College. Geneva! A block away. I missed his first evening lecture—Marty had come up to the house to go with me to his talk but we got distracted honing our newly discovered lovemaking skills; amazing how different it can be with the right person—but I went down the following evening for Woiwode's reading. Afterward I hung around and introduced myself, brother of W.D. Snodgrass—yes, of course I know De, how is he, please say hello for me, what are you doing here in Beaver Falls? I told him my situation, we exchanged addresses, and corresponded for a couple of years. In our exchanges I told him about my novel and that it was currently at his publisher, Farrar, Straus, and Giroux; he wrote back that he had asked his editor's assistant to find it in the slush pile and deliver it to Michael di Capua. Eventually, di Capua passed on it, but his assistant, Barbara, wrote to say how much she loved the book; she offered to help me find an agent, or that she would like to take the book with her as she started a new position as an editor at Viking. Gee, a young editor wants to take my book with her to one of the most prestigious publishing houses. It seemed like a no-brainer. True, she said she wasn't hired to be a fiction editor at Viking, she would be heading up a new division of glitzy lifestyle books, but Viking had assured her that she could be the editor of my fiction book. What could possibly go wrong?

Moving the Hat

Quite a lot, it turned out. I heard that for years after it was published, *There's Something in the Back Yard* was the subject of many a Friday night afterwork bar discussions among publishing types of Good Books That Should Have Made It and Didn't. The problem was that TSITBY became the victim of internecine jockeying between departments within the publisher, brought about because it wasn't being handled by an editor in the fiction department. It was particularly galling, apparently, because everyone who was involved with the book loved it and expected great things from it, I even received a note from the copy editor who said how much she enjoyed the book and called it magical. When it came time to present the book to the buyers, Barbara did what was said to be an exceptional presentation, building up enthusiasm for it. In an unexpected coup, TSITBY won the company's internal poll for the best fiction book to be released that year. Which turned out to be not a good thing. The company couldn't very well tout a book for which they only paid $7,000, over a new novel by one their premier authors for which they paid $45,000. The solution: they decided not to present the award at all that year. Even so, TSITBY seemed marked for success. The pre-pub reviews were impressive: a starred Kirkus Review called it "A striking debut." Publisher's Weekly said, "A haunting, seductive, original story." Best of all, The Washington Post Book World gave it half a page, second only to that week's feature book, the review saying, "Observe this mysterious book and be changed." Based on its early reception, a major paperback release was scheduled; and, the movie rights sold in the first week. I watched it all unfolding in front of me, thinking Wow, so this is how it happens. But. But the all-important New York Times review never came. Which was unexpected because Viking, anticipating the book's success, had hired a rep specially to nurse it through the system. Unfortunately, the guy they hired drank his lunch every day and disappeared in the afternoons; when they fired him two months later they found all the releases and follow-ups he should have sent in a desk drawer. By then it was too late, without the NYTimes review interest and sales for the book dropped off quickly; soon they cancelled the paperback edition, Viking wouldn't renew the movie rights. All gone.

Richard Snodgrass

Moving the Hat

Ted said it best. When he read in the paper that *There's Something in the Back Yard* was published, he called me from Beaver Falls: "So, let me get this straight, Snots. This book, you wrote every word of it?"

"Every word, Ted."

"All the *and's* and *the's* and *but's*?"

"Every single one. All the big words in between too."

Ted had to think about that for a moment. "So. What's next?"

"Not sure what you mean...."

"What's the next big thing? You published the book. Okay. So what happens next?"

"That's it. Now it's out of my hands."

Ted had to think about that too. "So. Time to get back to work."

Yes. Time to get back to work, not that I had ever stopped. Fortunately, over the years I had learned to deal with the disappointments and frustrations involved with being a writer, from the priest at St. Vincent who told me that he never saw any creativity in me, to the head of the writing program at Penn State who, when I applied for their MFA program while living in my mother's attic, not only rejected my application but went out of his way to say he didn't think I'd ever make a writer. But when you have the fire in you, it doesn't matter what others think. And I had the fire. My response to the sinking of *There's Something in the Back Yard* was to work even harder. I was already working on a new novel when I started at the ad agency; I was only hired part-time, six hours a day from ten to four, but I often stayed longer to get things finished, in reality working eight and ten hours a day, but those extra hours in the morning were precious to me. I had heard that Dan Rather, the newscaster, trained himself to function on five hours sleep a night; I figured if he could do it, so could I. Marty and I went to bed around nine at night but I'd be up by two, working through the wee hours with a short nap before getting Marty up, then working until it was time for me to leave as well. A schedule I still adhere to, the Elizabethan two-sleeps. As I write this now at three-thirty a.m., sitting in a circle of light with the darkness around me, the only time I feel I'm me.

Richard Snodgrass

Moving the Hat

I started my next novel while we were still living in Beaver Falls. I had long wanted to do a book about the construction of a high-rise building, after all I did know a few things about such an enterprise, but I soon realized that writing about a forty-story building could produce a book of a thousand pages. One thing I had noticed since I was back in the area was the number of mill towns that had a new ten- or twelve-story building sticking up in the middle of it, the result of redevelopment for affordable housing. Okay, why not reduce my book about a forty-story high-rise down to a dozen stories? That also worked into my desire to write about the area. I needed a mill town in which to place the building, and came up with the idea of Furnass, with a funny backstory about the wrong spelling of furnace, a place very much like Beaver Falls except with steeper streets and a domineering mill along the river. The storyline followed events and characters I had known in construction—it was nice to be around Jack Martin again—as well as people I knew from growing up in the area. But when I finished the book I felt I had some characters left over; there were characters in the fictitious town that had their own stories to tell that I felt deserved telling. What started out as one book became three, and the number of books about Furnass grew from there.

The problem with writing a series of novels without an overall plan, developing characters and storylines as you go along, is that you write the first book, get it into shape, then write the next—except that in writing the second book the characters and events from the first book may change. So after you finish the second book you have to go back and straighten out the first book, but that can change things about the second book so you have to rewrite it too. Then you start the third book but in the process things change about the first and second books, so you have to go back and—you get the idea. I think you can also see why, before I felt things were in final shape to start publishing the books as a series, it took thirty-five years. I was just grateful I had the thirty-five years to do them.

Moving the Hat

It's misleading, though, to say I waited thirty-five years before I tried to publish the books. Starting with *The Building*, then *Some Rise* and *All Fall Down*, I submitted them to one agent and then another, but things didn't go well. In one case, the agent had me come to his loft in New York City, playing The Clash at ear-splitting decibels as he returned to me all three manuscripts that he was supposedly shopping around, saying he wasn't interested anymore; unable to carry the boxes, I sat on the edge of a dumpster and tore up the pages. Another agent loved *The Building* but wanted to make severe edits; I said I would accept changes but I wanted to do the revisions myself. He sent me ten pages of changes he wanted before he'd represent the book. It took me a year but I finally got the manuscript into shape and sent it back to him. When I didn't hear anything in three months, I called him; he barely remembered me or the book, then remembered that with the changes he didn't like it.

After completing The Furnass Towers Trilogy, I got interested in a family who appeared in the books, the Lyles, and wrote a novel about them during the Civil War entitled *Across The River*. It's said you can't go wrong writing a Civil War novel, and I thought I finally had a book with popular appeal. I sent it to Herb Gold, whom I had known in San Francisco, who loved it and recommended it to his agent, Clyde Taylor, who was also Mario Puzo's agent. At last things were coming together. Clyde loved the book—he had passed on Charles Frazier's *Cold Mountain*, saying he loved *Across the River* more. The problem he encountered was that it wasn't Cold Mountain. One publisher would only take it if I rewrote it to be more like *Cold Mountain*. Another offered a minimal $6,000 with the stipulation that I come up with a family backstory on which it was based—you know, like *Cold Mountain*. Clyde reported these offers, but recommended I didn't take them. He said he had the same experience with *The Godfather*, he was sure he would find the right publisher. But after a year he gave up; he wrote that he didn't understand how he had failed but he was unable to sell my work and was ending the relationship. Best of luck.

Richard Snodgrass

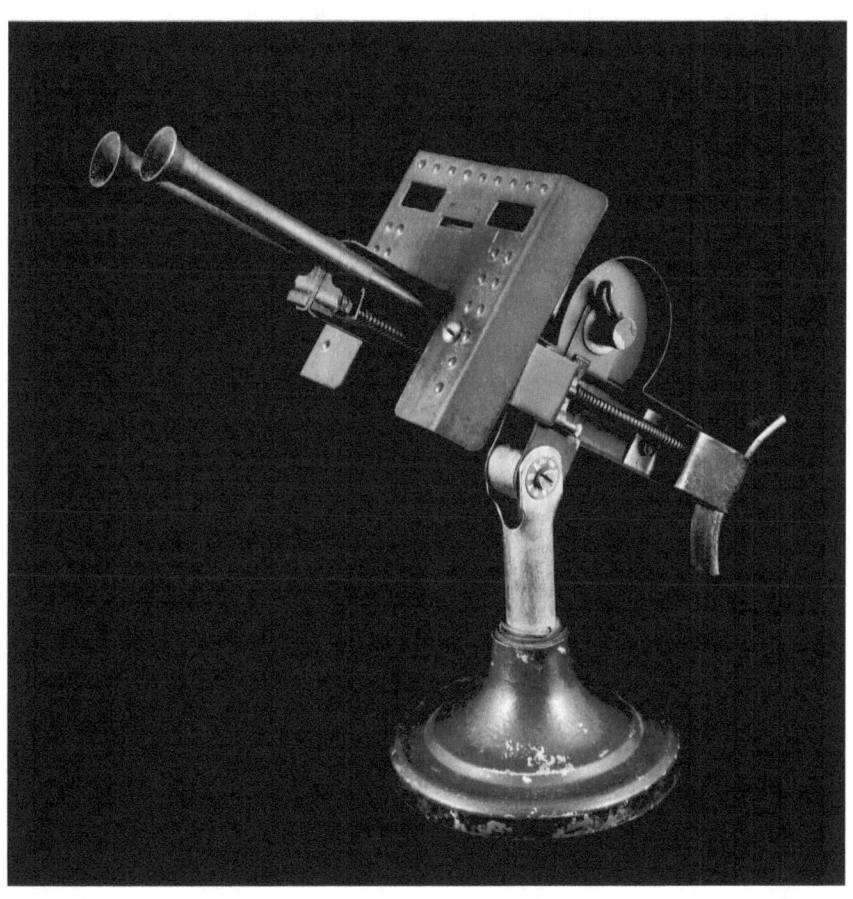

Moving the Hat

Finally, I had had enough. I had received one rejection too many. For the first time since I was in college, the fire went out; I gave up writing, I couldn't take any longer the frustrations, the put-downs, the feelings of failure. Enough.

"Maybe you could start to photograph again," Marty says. "You're really good at that and had a lot of success."

"Well, I was thinking about getting another Rollei. . . ."

"You need to do something, you're not Dick when you're not working," Marty says. Then adds under her breath, "plus, you're miserable to live with, no fun at all. . . ." She smiles, the Cheshire Cat.

For some time, I had seen what the art directors at the agency could do with some new software called Photoshop, and I thought you might be able to use those techniques to print photographs. Online I found a number of sites with more information, particularly one in Hong Kong, about the use of Epson printers and carbon-pigment inks, tricking the printer into thinking it was printing color while it was actually printing in shades of gray. In the evenings after everyone else had left I stayed at the agency and scanned the 4 x 5 negatives I had made during my LightWork fellowship to photograph the mill towns. At home with my own computer and Epson 1160 printer, I was able to make prints on watercolor paper that were indistinguishable from the platinum prints I had labored over in San Francisco.

I found a used Rollei SL66 Single-Lens Reflex on eBay, just like the one I had been forced to sell in order to finish TSITBY while living in my mother's attic. When it arrived and I unpacked it, we let the camera sit on the dining room table for a couple of days so she and I would be comfortable with each other; she told us her name was Rachel, after the Biblical Rachel searching for her children. Finally, one night after dinner, I loaded Rachel with a roll of Panatomic-X and, with Marty looking on, turned it toward the first image I saw, a shelf in the dining room china cabinet that Marty had arranged. On the groundglass I brought into focus a Wizard, a frog on a lily pad, and a trumping elephant, an image that talked to me of a new direction, full of wonder and magic and delight. My heart sang.

Richard Snodgrass

Moving the Hat

It was the start of a new century, and for a few years I concentrated on photography, taking time away from the agency to make field trips, spending my hours in the middle of the night processing negatives and making prints. Then a most amazing thing happened: the words returned. I put together a collection of my mill town images, along with sections of text, much as Wright Morris had done in *God's Country and My People*. The prose sections talked about my impressions of the area after being away for twenty years, along with my experiences making the photographs. The prose sections weren't meant to describe or caption the images; rather, they were written to stand alone, each its own brief narrative, the association with the image emotional, the prose a metaphor to the image, the image a metaphor to the prose. The first prose sections I did were limited to one-page each; as I got better at the form, I limited each narrative to approximately 400 words, constructed as tight as a sonnet. My mill town images and text became a one-man show entitled *Afterimage: Mill Life Remembered*, at Pittsburgh's Heinz History Center, an affiliate of the Smithsonian Institution. At the same time, the magazine *LensWork* printed selections of the images and text; when the article was later anthologized in *Looking at Images*, the editor, Brooks Jenkins, called the portfolio "one of the very best examples of a photo essay we've published." Mark Rengers Gallery in Sewickley, PA took an interest in my photographs and gave me a number of one-man shows, as well as taking on representing my work. While doing a presentation for the agency, I became aware of the Flight 93 temporary memorial in Shanksville, and began photographing the site, visiting it in all weathers and times of day, even in the middle of the night, for more than a year and a half; out of it came a book, *An Uncommon Field*, published by Carnegie Mellon University Press. Later I used a studio light-tent to photograph antique kitchen utensils, starting with the ones Marty brought from her farm-heritage in Southwestern Pennsylvania, which became a book, *Kitchen Things*, published by Skyhorse Publishing. For several years I photographed farms near Hickory, PA where Marty grew up, spending one day a week tramping around the fields and barns, Rachel and tripod slung over my shoulder. And then another most amazing thing happened: the stories of Furnass returned, too.

Richard Snodgrass

Moving the Hat

The time I spent working in advertising and public relations is a total mystery, a mystery how I got there to begin with—in an industry that I decried as often bordering on the immoral with its manipulations—a mystery as to how I did so well in it while I was there. And I was there quite a long time; as I write this I still do work for one client with my own little agency, thirty-six years after I began working for them. Go figure. One saving grace was that the first little agency that hired me was engaged primarily with business-to-business advertising; consumer advertising involves creating the sense of a lack in the consumer then offering a solution, whereas in business-to-business the subject is aware they lack something—materials, machines, something to help their business—and the advertising explains how the advertiser can supply it. Most "creatives" I encountered in agencies consider B-to-B the dregs, dry and boring and lacking in imagination, certainly not worthy of the artists they consider themselves to be. Sniff. For me it was an intellectual challenge, something to keep the mind active while sparing my imagination for my own work at night. I also considered working in the agency a spiritual exercise, to walk among them and not be part of them, and to never let them know—I was the guy with the hat and boots, my office lined with the dead balloons after Marty sent them to me, playing the Grateful Dead and ZZ Top as loud as I dared. Among my first clients was Pittsburgh's foremost civic leadership organization, which other writers avoided like the plague. I was fortunate the directors took a liking to me, and over the years when no one else wanted the work, I became not only the writer but the account rep and producer of videos and presentations, learning those skills as I went along by hiring the best people and treating them royally. There followed other clients, a major natural gas producer, downtown Pittsburgh's development organization, several divisions of Alcoa, to the extent that I was running an agency within the agency—the IT folks labeled me Snodgrass Industries. When my enemies within the company tried to reign me in, I decided I had had enough and quit--and what do you know, all my clients came with me. Snodgrass Industries, Inc., consisting of me and two cats, was born.

Richard Snodgrass

Moving the Hat

The stories of Furnass returned to me, slowly at first, almost begrudgingly, but insistent, refusing to leave me alone, demanding. I had been thinking of my brother, his latest work, *The Führer Bunker*, a series about Hitler and his associates' last days in the bunker. I didn't think the poems were very good, more intellectual exercises than felt emotion, but I was sure the emotion was there, somewhere, that De must be feeling like he was a man in a bunker, looking out through slits at the world as his enemies closed in on him, his critics, those who had begun to deprecate his work, ignore the influence he had on contemporary poetry, instead fussing over the other practitioners of the so-called Confessional School—Lowell, Sexton, Plath—saying he was a has-been, or worse, the cruelest blow, ignoring him completely. A man in a bunker. A man in a blockhouse. I began to put together the story of Furnass before there was a town there, the story of a lieutenant of the Black Watch, the lone survivor of a massacre, holed up in a blockhouse while outside there were Indians waiting to kill him. Or were there? After all he had been through—the massacre of the garrison, his escape through the woods, the isolation of being holed up in the blockhouse—perhaps he was only imagining his enemies, hallucinating; he had the growing realization that the only way to find out whether his demons were real or not was to walk through that door, go outside and confront whatever was or wasn't there. As I worked through those ideas, I realized I needed a frame for the story, and then a frame for the frame, layering the themes of balance and denial and awareness. I had long avoided first person narratives, preferring the omniscience of a third person narrator, but maybe writing in the first person would unblock my frustrations as a writer. Because I was aware that I was talking about a part of myself in the story of a man holed up. But for reasons I don't understand nor can take credit for, I felt it's not good enough to stay locked in your hideaway judging the world from your peepholes, waiting for the end. It's a measure of character to go through that door and find out what's actually out there and deal with it the best you can. Easy to say, of course.

Richard Snodgrass

Moving the Hat

A Book of Days, my story within a story within a story, is probably my most literary book, and close to my heart because of what it gave me, it was a breakthrough for me; like Lieutenant Keating I went through the door and realized that it didn't matter whether the work was recognized or not, it was my work, it was what I did, that was value enough to me, and I was going to keep doing it regardless. Henry James in *The Middle Years* said, "We work in the dark - we do what we can - we give what we have. Our doubt is our passion, and our passion is our task. The rest is the madness of art." A quote I had on a card tacked above my desk for years but never fully understood until I was ready to throw my work away and realized if I did I'd be throwing me away too. I maintained a balance of my photography with my writing, completing more of the Books of Furnass; the series reached ten books before I thought they were in sync enough with each other to try publishing them. I couldn't imagine a mainstream publisher taking on an entire series of books by an unknown author, and I hated to think of them spread out over multiple publishers and editions and formats—assuming that any of them got published at all. So in 2018 I started Calling Crow Press, subsidiary of Snodgrass Industries, Inc., and began the long and stumbling process of learning how to self-publish my books. I learned the pitfalls of book distribution when I self-published a reissue of my first novel, *There's Something in the Back Yard*. Accompanied by Jack Ritchie, my closet friend and colleague from years of doing client presentations, I went on the road again—moving the hat—on a book tour of the Southwest, a folly documented in a video *Travels with the Corn Dancer*. I also tried my hand at designing covers for the books. I showed them to Jack one day as we had a Guinness at the Harp and Fiddle; he took one look at what I'd come up with and declared he would do the covers for the books, "to save you from yourself." I undoubtedly could have used more of that in the course of my lifetime, but then I wouldn't have had as much fun, would I?

Richard Snodgrass

Moving the Hat

"Okay then," Marty says. "So you've wrapped up all the themes you started with, the importance of keeping your balance with your work and everyday life and with your art—and even within your art, the balance between your writing and your photography—as well as the balance between positive and negative energy, the plus and minus of all things, light and dark, right and wrong, each providing the opposition to define the other. You worked in the joys of being a Snodgrass, and even found ways to weave occasions of moving the hat around, nice."

"But I still haven't wrapped up the relationship with my brother."

Marty gives me a squinty-eyed look as if to say she was afraid I'd think of that.

After his letter about the copies of *Heart's Needle*, I didn't hear from De again. At one time I saw an announcement in the paper that he was giving a reading at Pitt; I was tempted to go, wondering how he'd handle it, but my better angels prevailed.

Then one day in 2009 I was gathering our empty garbage can from the curb when a neighbor, an accountant named J. J. who had always been impressed that I was the son of the revered accountant B. D. Snodgrass, pulled over beside me in his van.

"I saw in the paper that a writer named Snodgrass died," J.J. said, elbow out his window, "and I was wondering if it was you."

"Not that I know of, J. J."

"Do we need to ask Marty? Maybe she has an opinion."

"Cute." I picked up the lid from the grass, fitted it on the can. "You're a funny guy."

"So, you didn't know anything about his dying?"

"Nope, he didn't say a thing to me about it."

"You don't seem very upset."

I let it go at that. All I could think of was the line of one of De's poems about the death of our sister Barbara, that when he left her at her grave—which incidentally he never went to—he wouldn't spare one tear.

"That's bitter," Marty says.

"Yeah, I'm sorry to say. I never wished him ill, but there it is, I have to admit it. I think I'll go for a walk, clear the air. Want to come?"

"Wouldn't miss it for the world." She grabs the front door key, then looks back with a Marty grin. "Don't forget your hat."

Richard Snodgrass

# List of Images

PAGE

III	Frontispiece—At Ranchos de Taos, Winter 1976. Photographer: Brian Taylor.
VI	"Hardhat in Bookcase," from *Everything Ends or Changes*.
VIII	The hat and Guiness at Harp & Fiddle, Pittsburgh, PA.
3	"One-Eyed Teddy," from *Childish Things*.
5	"One-Eyed Teddy," Close-up, from *Childish Things*.
7	"Doggy Indian Club,: from *Childish Things*
9	"Headless Scottish Soldier," from *Childish Things*.
11	The hat on dashboard, location unknown.
13	The Brothers Snodgrass and Bozo the Clown during a visit to Beaver Falls, PA. Photographer: Helen Snodgrass.
15	"Ice Wagon," from *Childish Things*.
17	My father as a teenage iceman.
19	"Gyroscope at Rest," from *Childish Things*.
21	"Playhouse," from *Childish Things*.
23	My family's house, Beaver Falls, PA, October 1955. Photographer: Helen Snodgrass
25	My sisters: Shirley, with Gabriel; Barbara with Nanki Poo. Circa 1950, from *The House with Round Windows*
27	"Swing," from *Childish Things*.
29	Collage: Growing Up.
31	"Drummer Bear,: from *Childish Things*.
33	Drum solo at Prom, 1958, photographer unknown.
35	"Shirley Temple Doll," from *Childish Things*.
37	"Slag Cars and Mill," from *When There Was Steel*.
39	"Mary in the Weeds," from *When There Was Steel*.
41	"Flopsie Rabbit," from *Childish Things*.
43	"Joann's Grandmother." 1958.
45	"Angel and Flag," from *When There Was Steel*.
47	"Blind Mary," from *Images from a Small Space*.
49	"Tin Trolley," from *Childish Things*.
51	"Casper, The Friendly Ghost,:" from *Childish Things*.
53	"Christ on a Wall," from *When There Was Steel*.

55 "St. Mary's Before a Storm," from *When There Was Steel*.
57 "Draft Poem on a Napkin" by W. D. Snodgrass. Detroit, Winter 1961
59 "Bill's Toy," from *Childish Things*.
60 PPS to a letter from W. D. Snodgrass to Richard Snodgrass, Spring 1958.
61 "Bill's Toy," close-up, from *Childish Things*.
63 Nathan Oliveira, Standing Man with Stick, 1959. New Images of Man, Peter Selz, The Modern Museum of Art, New York, 1959.
65 "Tin Airplane," from *Childish Things*.
67 "Pick-Up Sticks Falling," from *Childish Things*.
69 "Pick-Up Sticks Fallen," from *Childish Things*.
71 "The Rocking Horse Winner," from *Childish Things*.
73 From a letter from W. D. Snodgrass, July 8 ?, 1965 [?].
75 Poster for The Flying Wallenda's, date unknown.
77 "Doll Circle with Fallen Member, Japanese Miniature Dolls," from *Childish Things*.
79 With Roger Perkins, Larry Perkins, and Halsey Brant, Sutro Heights Park, Summer 1963. Photographer unknown.
81 "Yoyo," from *Childish Things*.
83 "Japanese Miniature Dolls," from *Childish Things*.
85 "Spirit of '76," Flat Lead Soldiers,, from *Childish Things*.
87 "Plastic Tank with Bobbing Driver," from *Childish Things*.
89 3x5 Card with Castaneda Reminders.
91 "Tinker Toys, from *Childish Things*.
93 "Erector Set by Gilbert," from *Childish Things*.
95 "Dump Truck," from *Childish Things*.
97 "Blind Teddy," from *Childish Things*.
99 "Jigsaw," from *Childish Things*.
101 "Jigsaw," detail, from *Childish Things*.
103 "Fred," from *Images in a Small Space*.
105 Collage: Construction.
107 "Hat on Coat Tree," from *Everything Ends or Changes*.
109 "Kennel Dog," from *Childish Things*.
111 "JoAnn's Doll," from *Childish Things*.
113 "Marionettes," from *Childish Things*.
115 Collage: from *Everything Ends or Changes*.

117 Draft of Untitled Poem, W. D. Snodgrass, Circa 1965
119 "Bambi and Flower," from *Childish Things*.
121 "Roller Dog," from *Childish Things*.
123 "Befuddle Dog," from *Childish Things*.
125 "Window Tree," from *Erieville*.
127 Collage: from *Erieville*.
129 "Dog and Butterfly," from *Childish Things*.
131 "Pillows," from *Everything Ends or Changes*.
133 "Stereopticon and Card with Angel," from *Childish Things*.
135 "Faceless Doll," from *Childish Things*.
137 "Fallen Top," from *Childish Things*.
139 "Dining Room in the Afternoon, " from *The House with Round Windows*.
141 Collage: from *The House with Round Windows*.
143 "House, Chair, Tree," from *Erieville*.
145 "Crayon Set," from *Childish Things*.
147 "Kewpie Doll," from *Childish Things*.
149 "Rocket Car," from *Childish Things*.
151 "Living Room, Before and After," from *Everything Ends or Changes*.
153 Sketch on a Napkin, by an Unknown Artist at a Denny's.
155 "Airplane Girl," from *Childish Things*.
157 "Playhouse with the Lid Off," from *Childish Things*.
159 "Owl in the Shed, from *Erieville*.
161 "Box of Miniature Dolls," from *Childish Things*.
163 Collage: from *Erieville* (exteriors).
165 "Sweater," from *When There Was Steel*.
167 "Letter Blocks, Stacked," from *Childish Things*.
169 "Design Blocks, Jumbled," from *Childish Things*.
171 "Design Blocks, Arranged, With One Missing," from *Childish Things*.
173 House at Wurlitzer Foundation, Taos, NM
175 "The Great Feathered Stetson," from *Everything Ends or Changes*.
177 "Corn Dancer," from *Childish Things*.

179 "Corn Dancer," Closeup, from *Childish Things*.
181 "Parakeet Kachina," made by Jason and MacKenzie Tuttle, *Childish Things*.
183 "Parakeet Kachina", Closeup, made by Jason and MacKenzie Tuttle, *Childish Things*.
185 "Firetruck Driver, Headed East," from *Childish Things*.
187 "Firetruck Driver, Headed West, from *Childish Things*.
189 "Third Floor Stairs," from *The House with Round Windows*.
191 The Hat on the bar, Stratford, Ontario.
193 "Three soldiers in Air Raid," from *Childish Things*.
195 "Handmade Pull Toy," from *Childish Things*.
197 "Atomic Flash," from *Childish Things*.
199 "Jigsaw Puzzle, Jumbled," from *Childish Things*.
201 "Jigsaw Puzzle Pieces, Lovers," from *Childish Things*.
203 "Flower," from *Childish Things*.
205 "Helen's Spring Hats," from *The House with Round Windows*.
206 Mother's unsent note to De, date unknown.
207 Letter from W. D. Snodgrass, March 18, 1988.
209 "Wheeled Mouse," from *Childish Things*.
211 "Wood Locomotive with Figure," from *Childish Things*.
213 Cover, *There's Something in the Back Yard*.
215 "Ball and Jacks," from *Childish Things*.
217 "Wood Carousel," from *Childish Things*.
219 Map of Furnass.
221 "Antiaircraft 'Pom-Pom' Gun," from *Childish Things*.
223 "Wizard, Elephant, and Frog," from *Images from a Small Space*.
225 Collage: *When There Was Steel*; *An Uncommon Field*; *Kitchen Things*.
227 "Supermarket and Scales," from *Childish Things*.
229 "Flat Lead Soldiers Attack an Indian in the Land of Oz," from *Images from a Small Space*.
231 The Hat on a Statue with a Bian Taylor Landscape, from *Images from a Small Space*.
233 "Helen and Heart's Needle," from *Images from a Small Space*.
232 "Electric Candle in the Window," from *Images from a Small Space*.

Richard Snodgrass' series of novels and short stories, The Books of Furnass, about a fictitious Western Pennsylvania mill town, was released beginning in 2018. He is also the author of the novel, *There's Something in the Back Yard*, Viking Press, 1989; two books of photographs and text: *An Uncommon Field: The Flight 93 Temporary Memoria*l, published in September of 2011 by Carnegie Mellon University Press; and, *Kitchen Things: An Album of Vintage Utensils*, published in 2013 by Skyhorse, named one of the year's "best books to get you thinking about food" by the Associated Press. In 2022, Carnegie Mellon University Press published a memoir entitled, *The House with Round Windows*.

Richard Snodgrass's short stories and essays have appeared in the *New England Review/Bread Loaf Quarterly*, *South Dakota Review*, *California Review*, *Pittsburgh Quarterly*, and elsewhere. He is also a master photographer who has been artist-in-residence at LightWorks (University of Syracuse) and at the Helene Wurlitzer Foundation in Taos, New Mexico. He is the recipient of a fellowship from the Pennsylvania Council on the Arts.

Richard Snodgrass lives in Pittsburgh, PA with his wife Marty and two indomitable female tuxedo cats, raised from feral kittens, named Frankie and Becca.

For more information, go to RichardSnodgrass.com

www.ingramcontent.com/pod-product-compliance
Lightning Source LLC
Chambersburg PA
CBHW022015120526
44580CB00015B/109/J